ESSENTIAL
REPTILES

by K. A. Hale

CONTENT CONSULTANT

Joseph R. Mendelson III, PhD
Director of Research, Zoo Atlanta
Adjunct Associate Professor
School of Biology, Georgia Institute of Technology

ESSENTIAL
ANIMALS

Essential Library

An Imprint of Abdo Publishing
abdobooks.com

abdobooks.com

Published by Abdo Publishing, a division of ABDO, PO Box 398166, Minneapolis, Minnesota 55439. Copyright © 2022 by Abdo Consulting Group, Inc. International copyrights reserved in all countries. No part of this book may be reproduced in any form without written permission from the publisher. Essential Library™ is a trademark and logo of Abdo Publishing.

Printed in the United States of America, North Mankato, Minnesota.
102021
012022

Cover Photos: Eric Isselee/Shutterstock Images, (alligator), (Komodo dragon); Shutterstock Images, (Gila monster), (sea turtle); Lukas Gojda/Shutterstock Images, (chameleon); Kit Thanit/Shutterstock Images, (cobra)

Interior Photos: Lukas Gojda/Shutterstock Images, 1; Huy Thoai/Shutterstock Images, 4; Elliotte Rusty Harold/Shutterstock Images, 7; Chantelle Bosch/Shutterstock Images, 8; Shutterstock Images, 10, 26, 36, 48, 76, 102 (Gila monster), 102 (softshell turtle); Narupon Nimpaiboon/Shutterstock Images, 11; Faiz Zaki/Shutterstock Images, 12; Alexey Pelikh/iStockphoto, 13; iStockphoto, 14, 44, 50–51, 58, 59, 72, 80, 92, 102 (snapping turtle), 103 (gharial), 103 (sea turtle), 103 (crocodile); Bildagentur Zoonar GmbH/Shutterstock Images, 16; Eric Isselee/Shutterstock Images, 16–17, 44–45, 93, 102 (rattlesnake); Ekaterina Kamenetsky/Shutterstock Images, 18 (left), 102 (alligator); Sanit Fuangnakhon/Shutterstock Images, 18 (right); John Serrao/Science Source, 19; Pong Wira/Shutterstock Images, 20, 103 (blind snake); Joseph T. and Suzanne L. Collins/Science Source, 22; Michael Benard/Shutterstock Images, 22–23; Matt Jeppson/Shutterstock Images, 24, 38 (right), 77, 102 (kingsnake); E. R. Degginger/Science Source, 27; I Wayan Sumatika/Shutterstock Images, 28; Scott Linstead/Science Source, 30, 91, 102 (flying dragon); Corina Sturm/Shutterstock Images, 31; Jay Ondreicka/Shutterstock Images, 32, 102 (glass lizard); Patrick K. Campbell/Shutterstock Images, 34; Belle Ciezak/Shutterstock Images, 38 (left); Ken Griffiths/Shutterstock Images, 39, 103 (long-necked turtle); Rodrigo Buendia/AFP/Getty Images, 40, 102 (tortoise); Red Line Editorial, 42, 102–103; Pablo Cozzaglio/AFP/Getty Images, 43; Michel Gunther/Science Source, 47; Rusty Dodson/Shutterstock Images, 49; Niki Cruz/iStockphoto, 52; Francois Gohier/Science Source, 53, 102 (anaconda); Jany Sauvanet/Science Source, 54; M. Watson/Science Source, 56; Sibons Photography/Shutterstock Images, 60, 103 (cobra); Yashpal Rathore/NaturePL/Science Source, 61; Mufti Adi Utomo/Shutterstock Images, 63; Sergey Uryadnikov/Shutterstock Images, 64, 103 (Komodo dragon); K. Kaplan/iStockphoto, 65; Fletcher & Baylis/Science Source, 67, 83; Ken Thomas/Science Source, 68; John A. Anderson/Shutterstock Images, 69; Curioso Photography/Shutterstock Images, 70, 102 (painted turtle); Iakov Filimonov/Shutterstock Images, 73; ANT Photo Library/Science Source, 75; Ryan M. Bolton/Shutterstock Images, 79; Roman Teteruk/Shutterstock Images, 81, 103 (gecko); Vladislav T. Jirousek/Shutterstock Images, 84; Mark Boulton/Science Source, 85; B. G. Thomson/Science Source, 86–87, 103 (tuatara); Kuttelvaserova Stuchelova/Shutterstock Images, 88, 103 (chameleon); Kaan Sezer/iStockphoto, 90; Audrey Snider-Bell/Shutterstock Images, 95; Ed Crisostomo/The Orange County Register/AP Images, 96; Ken Griffiths/iStockphoto, 97, 102 (sea snake); Auscape/Universal Images Group/Getty Images, 98

Editor: Arnold Ringstad
Series Designer: Sarah Taplin

Library of Congress Control Number: 2020949050

Publisher's Cataloging-in-Publication Data

Names: Hale, K. A., author.
Title: Essential reptiles / by K. A. Hale
Description: Minneapolis, Minnesota : Abdo Publishing, 2022 | Series: Essential animals | Includes online resources and index.
Identifiers: ISBN 9781532195556 (lib. bdg.) | ISBN 9781098215934 (ebook)
Subjects: LCSH: Reptiles--Juvenile literature. | Reptiles--Behavior--Juvenile literature. | Animals--Identification--Juvenile literature. | Zoology--Juvenile literature.
Classification: DDC 598.1--dc23

CONTENTS

INTRODUCTION 4

ALLIGATOR SNAPPING TURTLE 12

AMERICAN ALLIGATOR 16

BRAHMINY BLIND SNAKE................................20

CALIFORNIA KINGSNAKE................................24

COMMON FLYING DRAGON..............................28

EASTERN GLASS LIZARD................................32

EASTERN LONG-NECKED TURTLE 36

ESPAÑOLA GIANT TORTOISE..........................40

GHARIAL 44

GILA MONSTER 48

GREEN ANACONDA...52

GREEN SEA TURTLE.......................................56

KING COBRA...60

KOMODO DRAGON 64

PAINTED TURTLE 68

SALTWATER CROCODILE 72

SPINY SOFTSHELL TURTLE............................76

TOKAY GECKO..80

TUATARA 84

VEILED CHAMELEON 88

WESTERN DIAMONDBACK RATTLESNAKE 92

YELLOW-BELLIED SEA SNAKE........................96

ESSENTIAL FACTS   100
REPTILES AROUND THE WORLD   102
GLOSSARY   104
ADDITIONAL RESOURCES   106

SOURCE NOTES   108
INDEX   110
ABOUT THE AUTHOR   112
ABOUT THE CONSULTANT   112

Reptiles have inspired myths and legends throughout human history.

Humans have been intrigued and terrified by reptiles for thousands of years. They are found in legends and cultures around the world. Chinese art depicting dragons dates back to 4500 BCE. The Aztec god of wind and rain was called Quetzalcoatl, which means "feathered serpent," and was often depicted as part bird, part snake. The naga of Hinduism and Buddhism takes a half-human, half-cobra form.

Fearsome reptiles of mythology include the basilisk, a giant serpent that can kill with a single glance, and Gorgons, women with snakes for hair.

But the reptiles of reality are just as awe-inspiring as those of legend. For more than 100 million years, reptiles ruled the earth. Dinosaurs roamed the land, ichthyosaurs and plesiosaurs swam in the sea, and pterosaurs soared through the air. Though the last of these fearsome creatures went extinct 66 million years ago, today's reptiles are descended from them. There are almost 10,000 known living species of reptiles, and scientists may yet discover more.[1]

Humans have coexisted with reptiles for millennia. People keep lizards, turtles, and snakes as pets. But this coexistence has not always been peaceful. American alligators were hunted nearly to extinction until governments made laws to protect them. Reptiles are killed so their skins can be used for fashion items, such as handbags, shoes, and belts. Reptiles also suffer from the effects of climate change and habitat loss. Many people kill reptiles out of fear. According to zoology professor Tom Kemp, "Wild reptiles are more badly affected than other organisms due to a variety of cultural practices and misunderstandings. . . . Enlightened education of the next generation is the best way to overcome such prejudice."[2]

FUN FACT

Birds are also technically reptiles, even though they are often considered separately. In fact, birds and crocodilians evolved from a common ancestor.

REPTILE BODIES

Lizards, snakes, crocodiles, and turtles are all reptiles, and they represent a great diversity in size, form, and behavior. But reptiles do share a few traits. All reptiles have scales. Scales are made of a protein called keratin, which is also found in rhinoceros horns, bird feathers, and human fingernails. Scales act as a sort of armor, protecting reptiles' skin and preventing water loss. Unlike fish scales, a reptile's scales cannot be easily scraped off. Some species have spikes or horns made from scales. The scales of lizards and snakes are small and allow the body to flex. Turtles and crocodiles are covered in large plates called scutes. In crocodiles, many of the scales contain large pieces of bone that create very durable protection. In most turtles and tortoises, scutes on the body fuse together to cover the bony shell. Scales contain the pigments that create an animal's coloration. Other reptiles have pigment cells in the skin. Coloration in reptiles can help animals blend in with their surroundings, warn off predators, or attract mates.

Reptiles are ectothermic, which means they cannot regulate body temperature internally. Instead, they must take heat from the environment around them. One way they do this is by basking in the sun. A reptile will often lie in the sun in the early morning, absorbing heat as the day gets warmer. When the reptile reaches

REPTILE EXTREMES

The nearly 10,000 species of reptiles vary greatly in size, appearance, and shape. The largest snake is the reticulated python, which can grow up to 33 feet (10 m) long. The smallest is the thread snake, which grows only up to 4.5 inches (11.4 cm) long. The Komodo dragon is the largest and heaviest lizard, measuring in at up to 10 feet (3 m) long and 176 pounds (80 kg). The dwarf gecko is the smallest at 0.63 inches (1.6 cm) and 0.004 ounces (0.12 g).[3] Size is not the only notable reptile extreme. Galápagos tortoises have incredibly long life spans, at more than 100 years. One tortoise was recorded as being 171 years old.[4]

Reptiles are commonly seen basking in the sun for warmth.

its ideal body temperature, it then seeks shade to avoid overheating. Some species have additional ways of regulating temperature, such as slowing down the heart rate or changing skin color.

REPTILE BEHAVIOR

Reptiles move in a variety of ways. They scurry, climb, jump, swim, or slither. Lizards and crocodiles flex their bodies side to side and push backward with their limbs. Snakes often use lateral motion too, but they don't have limbs to move them forward. The large scales on a snake's belly help it gain traction with the ground. In addition to lateral movement,

Lacking the legs that most land animals have, snakes use unique methods to move through their environments.

snakes in tight spaces can move like accordions, compressing tightly and then stretching out. Some snakes that live in sandy areas can sidewind. In this maneuver, a snake flexes its body laterally and also vertically, creating two alternating waves of motion down the body. This creates a looping movement that propels the snake in a sideways direction. This allows the snake to move without slipping in the loose sand. A turtle's shell prevents it from using lateral movement like other reptiles. Turtles rely on their limbs to move around. Marine turtles have limbs that work well as paddles but are less useful on land.

CLASSIFYING REPTILES

Scientists classify life in a series of increasingly specific groups. From broadest to narrowest, these groups are domain, kingdom, phylum, class, order, family, genus, and species. Reptiles are part of the kingdom Animalia, which includes all animals. They are in the phylum Chordata, which contains mostly vertebrates. Reptiles belong to the class Reptilia.

Living reptiles, not including birds, are divided into four orders. Squamata is the order for lizards and snakes. This order has the most species, with more than 9,000 members. Testudines, sometimes called Chelonia, contains turtles and tortoises. It includes about 340 species. The order Crocodylia contains crocodiles, alligators, and gharials, and it has around 25 species. Finally, Rhynchocephalia contains a single living species: the tuatara from New Zealand.[5] Each species has a unique scientific name, made up of its genus and species. For example, the American alligator's scientific name is *Alligator mississippiensis*.

Today's crocodiles and alligators look similar to their ancestors from 200 million years ago.

Snakes can wrap themselves around branches, allowing them to hunt in trees or escape from predators.

ESSENTIAL REPTILES

This book presents 22 notable reptile species from around the world. The species are presented alphabetically by their common names. These reptiles represent the amazing diversity in size, behavior, and appearance of the class Reptilia. Some are commonly seen as pets, such as the painted turtle. Some, such as the saltwater crocodile, are deadly predators. Narrative stories, colorful photos, fact boxes, and the latest scientific findings help bring to life the scaly creatures that have fascinated people throughout human history.

The alligator snapping turtle has distinctive sharp ridges on its shell.

A 50-pound (23 kg) alligator snapping turtle lies at the bottom of a creek in Louisiana. Its spiny shell looks like a log in the murky water. It can hold its breath for almost an hour. The alligator snapping turtle is an ambush predator. This means it does not chase its prey. Instead, it slowly opens its mouth. Then it stays perfectly still. Sooner or later, dinner will come to it.

The alligator snapping turtle has a unique feature on its tongue. A pink protrusion that looks like a worm sticks out from the end. The turtle wiggles this lure in the water.

The lure will help it catch a meal. The turtle mostly eats fish, but it also eats frogs, snails, snakes, insects, and even other turtles. Soon a fish comes along. The fish examines the lure in the turtle's mouth. The turtle holds perfectly still, moving only the lure. Soon, the fish's hunger wins out. It bites down on the lure. Quick as a blink, the turtle snaps its jaws shut, killing the fish. The alligator snapping turtle's powerful jaws can easily cut through meat and bone.

FUN FACT

Alligator snapping turtles have a bite force of more than 1,000 pounds per square inch (6,900 kPa).[7]

APPEARANCE AND BEHAVIOR

The alligator snapping turtle is the largest freshwater turtle in North America.[6] Males weigh an average of 175 pounds (80 kg), though they can exceed 200 pounds (90 kg). Females are smaller. The turtle's brown color and ridged carapace allow it to blend in with logs and rocks in murky waters.

The alligator snapping turtle is known for its powerful jaws, but like

Alligator snapping turtles lie in wait for their prey.

all turtles, it has no teeth. Its upper and lower jaws are made of keratin plates. These plates can keep growing, so they do not break down like teeth would. They form a sharp beak that allows an alligator snapper to slice its prey in two. If a person handles one of these turtles carelessly, the bite is powerful enough to remove a finger.

Alligator snappers spend the majority of their lives in the water. Like other aquatic turtles, they have lost the ability to pull their heads and limbs into their shells. Female alligator snappers come on land to lay their eggs. They dig nests around 160 feet (49 m) from the water and lay anywhere from eight to 52 eggs. After that, turtle parents don't have anything to do with their offspring. The baby turtles are independent when they hatch.

SUPER SENSES AND MORE

As with other aquatic turtles, alligator snapping turtles have a special way of finding their prey. An alligator snapper can pump water into and out of its throat. It tests the water for chemicals released by its prey. Essentially, the turtle can taste signs that its prey is nearby. The turtle can then search for food.

Full-grown alligator snappers have no natural predators, though eggs and young turtles can be eaten by alligators, birds, raccoons, and large fish. Humans are the only real threats to adult alligator snappers. People hunt them for their shells and meat. They also sell them illegally in the exotic pet trade. The turtles are classified as a vulnerable species. As a result, US states have protections in place for alligator snapping turtles. Commercial harvest of alligator snappers is completely illegal in Louisiana.

ALLIGATOR SNAPPING TURTLE
Macrochelys temminckii

SIZE
2.2 feet (66 cm) long on average for males; females are smaller

WEIGHT
Males 175 pounds (80 kg) on average; females up to 50 pounds (23 kg)

RANGE
Southeastern United States, as far north as Illinois and Kansas

HABITAT
Freshwater rivers, lakes, swamps

DIET
Mostly fish, also other turtles, mollusks, snakes, frogs, snails, worms, insects, crayfish, clams, aquatic plants

LIFE SPAN
11–45 years for males; 15–37 years for females

American alligators can breathe and see while remaining mostly submerged.

"**F**ore!" The woman swings her golf club, then shields her eyes against the sun as she watches the ball sail across the green. It lands near one of the many ponds on the golf course. As she gets closer, she stops. She isn't the only one on the course.

An American alligator lurks in the water. Another is on the shore, attempting to enter the pond. But the larger gator in the water has other thoughts. He smacks his head against the surface of the pond, sending up a huge splash. The smaller gator stops, but he doesn't leave. The bigger gator lunges out of the water, snapping his jaws at the smaller one. The smaller gator moves away; this is not a fight he would win.

The larger gator settles back into the water. His throat swells. He lets out a low, deep growl called a bellow. The vibrations through his body are so intense that the water above his back begins to dance, forming shapes on the surface. The bellow has a dual purpose. The gator is telling other males to stay away from his territory. He is also calling out to nearby female gators. If a female is impressed by his bellow, she may bellow back.

LARGE AND IN CHARGE

The American alligator is the largest reptile in the United States. Native to North America, it can be found in the marshy areas of the southeastern United States, especially in Florida and Louisiana. The average length of an American alligator is 11.5 feet (3.5 m), but gators can grow to more than 14 feet (4.3 m). Their tails account for more than half of this length. The powerful tail helps a gator move quickly and easily through the water, reaching speeds of up to 20 miles per hour (32 kmh).[8]

Perhaps the most distinctive feature of the American alligator is its jaws. The jaws are strong enough to crack a turtle's shell. They are lined with 80 sharp teeth.[9] If an American alligator loses a tooth, a new one will grow to fill its place. A gator can go through thousands of teeth in its lifetime. After capturing its prey, sometimes bringing it into the water to drown, an alligator will use its teeth to rip chunks of flesh off its prey and swallow them whole. It also swallows stones to crush and grind up its food, aiding in digestion.

FUN FACT

The largest recorded American alligator was 14.3 feet (4.4 m) long and weighed 900 pounds (408 kg). It was found in Jackson County, Texas, in 1998.[10]

ALLIGATOR VS. CROCODILE

ALLIGATOR

Rounded snout

Back teeth tuck into mouth when closed

Usually gray or black

CROCODILE

Pointed snout

Back lower teeth jut out over jaw

Usually tan or olive green

HUMAN INTERACTION

American alligators are naturally afraid of humans, but when people feed alligators illegally, gators may lose that fear. They may associate people with food. Gators can be found on golf courses and in swimming pools. While gators can be dangerous to humans, they do not often attack unprovoked. Females become territorial when guarding their nests, but they usually give intruders a warning by hissing, allowing intruders to move away. According to the Florida Fish and Wildlife Conservation Commission, there were only 421 unprovoked alligator bites from 1948 to 2020. A bite is considered unprovoked when a person was not harassing or handling a wild gator but still was bitten. Of those 421, only 26 bites were fatal.[11] A person has only an approximately 1 in 3.1 million chance of being seriously injured in an unprovoked gator attack in Florida.[12]

AMERICAN ALLIGATOR
Alligator mississippiensis

SIZE
11.5 feet (3.5 m) on average

WEIGHT
200–900 pounds (91–408 kg)

RANGE
Southeastern United States, as far west as Texas and Oklahoma and as far north as North Carolina

HABITAT
Wetlands, marshes, swamps, lakes, ponds, rivers, streams

DIET
Fish, amphibians, reptiles, birds, mammals

LIFE SPAN
20–30 years in the wild; approximately 50 years in captivity

At first glance, the Brahminy blind snake may look like a worm.

A man in Florida kneels by his flower bed, wiping the sweat from his brow. He is nearly finished planting his garden for the year. Having dug a hole for the next plant, he reaches for a pot, pulling out the plant and separating the soil at its roots. He startles when he notices a dark shape wiggling around in the soil. He grabs it gently, pulling it loose. *Probably an earthworm*, he thinks, ready to release it into the soil of his garden. But he stops, looking more closely. Earthworms have segmented bodies, and this creature is completely smooth. It is covered in tiny, dark scales. The two ends look similar, but one end has a little spike.

The creature presses it into his hand. It doesn't hurt, but it does release a foul smell. As the man looks closely at the other end, he sees a little forked tongue. This isn't an earthworm— it's a snake!

The man snaps a picture with his phone before putting the plant back in the pot with the snake. It burrows quickly into the soil. He sends the picture to a friend who studies snakes, asking whether she knows what it is. She says it looks like a Brahminy blind snake, a harmless, nonvenomous snake. It probably came from far away, a stowaway nestled in the flower pot. But she urges him to keep it if he can—scientists like her are eager to find specimens to study. She says she'll be over to pick it up as soon as possible.

WORLD TRAVELER

The Brahminy blind snake is the most widely distributed terrestrial reptile in the world. Native to India, Sri Lanka, and Southeast Asia, this snake can now be found in at least 118 countries in Asia, Europe, North America, Africa, and Australia.[13] Its nickname is the flowerpot snake—a name that helps explain its wide distribution throughout the world. The tiny, burrowing snake gets transported around the world in the soil of potted plants. As long as there is enough food in the soil for it to eat, it can live comfortably in a flowerpot. The Brahminy blind snake is nearly completely blind. It has tiny eyes that it can use only to distinguish between light and darkness.

FUN FACT
A Brahminy blind snake turns blue when it is about to shed its skin.

UNIQUE REPRODUCTION

Once it arrives, the Brahminy blind snake has an advantage in starting a new population. It is a parthenogenetic snake species. This means all Brahminy blind snakes are female, and they reproduce without a male. Most other species must find another member of the species in order to reproduce. This makes it impossible to establish a new population if one member is accidentally transported out of its home range. Since the Brahminy blind snake can reproduce on its own, one snake can create a new population if the habitat has the right conditions. This is how the Brahminy blind snake came to live around the world.

Scientists in Japan studied the reproductive biology of 49 Brahminy blind snakes found on the Ryukyu archipelago in Japan. They found that the snakes laid clutches of one to six eggs that were 0.4 to 0.8 inches (1.1–2 cm) long and weighed only 0.004 to 0.008 ounces (0.12–0.23 g)—about the weight of a raindrop.[14]

BRAHMINY BLIND SNAKE
Indotyphlops braminus

SIZE
4.4–6.5 inches (11.2–16.5 cm) long

WEIGHT
Less than 0.04 ounces (1 g)

RANGE
Native to India, Sri Lanka, Southeast Asia; introduced worldwide

HABITAT
Warm areas with moist soil; often found in gardens, rotting logs, natural debris

DIET
Ant and termite eggs, pupae, larvae

LIFE SPAN
Unavailable

The California kingsnake lacks venom, instead using its overwhelming strength to squeeze prey to death.

CALIFORNIA KINGSNAKE

The California kingsnake slithers quickly through the dry desert grass. Suddenly it stops. The telltale rattling sound of a rattlesnake fills the air. A rattlesnake's venom makes it a fearsome predator. But the nonvenomous kingsnake can be deadly too. Kingsnakes are constrictors—the strongest constrictors in the world, according to some scientists. They don't need venom to take down their prey when they can squeeze an animal to death by stopping its blood flow. And the California kingsnake has a secret weapon against this rattlesnake. Proteins in its body make it resistant to rattlesnake venom.

The kingsnake approaches the rattler, its forked tongue darting in and out of its mouth. Before the rattlesnake can open its jaws to strike, the California kingsnake clamps its own jaws around the rattler's head and tightly wraps its body around the rattler. The rattlesnake thrashes, trying to escape the kingsnake. But the kingsnake is nearly twice as long as the rattlesnake. The rattlesnake's tail continues to thrash. Its movement grows slower and slower until it finally stops. The kingsnake swallows the rattlesnake's head, then slowly swallows the rest of the body, eating the rattlesnake alive.

APPEARANCE AND HABITAT

California kingsnakes are a polymorphic species. Polymorphism is when two or more distinct colors or patterns can occur in a single population of a species. Predators are often familiar with only one of the patterns, or morphs, which improves the survival rate of the other morph. When one pattern becomes less common than the other, predators will turn their focus to the other. The most common morph of the California kingsnake is black or brown with white or cream bands down the body. Another common morph is the striped California kingsnake, which has stripes running down the length of its body. There are many variations of these two basic morphs.

FUN FACT

The California kingsnake is one of the most popular snake species to own as a pet.

Despite the name, California kingsnakes live beyond the confines of California. They can also be found in southwestern Oregon, Nevada, southern Utah, Arizona, and northwestern Mexico. They thrive in deserts and other dry places.

SNAKE EATER

Aside from occasional defensive bites, California kingsnakes are harmless

A striped California kingsnake

to humans. Their ability to eat venomous snakes makes them valuable for keeping populations of those snakes in check. A mechanism called cranial kinesis is important to many kinds of snakes, including the kingsnake. A snake's upper jaws can hinge upward as its lower jaws hinge downward. This allows it to open its mouth extremely wide, sometimes as much as 180 degrees. Compared to other vertebrates, snakes have additional bones with loose connections in their jaw systems, so they can spread their jaws apart easily. This allows a snake to eat prey that is larger than its head. Because they are not connected together, the left and right jaws can also move individually. Once a snake has taken its prey into its mouth, the left and right jaws work alternately to pull the prey down its throat. The California kingsnake's ability to eat snakes larger than itself and its immunity to venom make it a formidable predator.

CALIFORNIA KINGSNAKE
Lampropeltis californiae

SIZE
3.5 feet (1.1 m)

WEIGHT
3 pounds (1.3 kg)

RANGE
California, southwestern Oregon, Nevada, southern Utah, Arizona, northwestern Mexico

HABITAT
Rocky hillsides, deserts, arid places, forests, meadows, land used for agriculture

DIET
Other snakes, rodents, fish, lizards, frogs, birds

LIFE SPAN
20 years in the wild

The brightly colored dewlap under the neck is an instantly recognizable feature of the common flying dragon.

A common flying dragon climbs a tree in Indonesia. It is looking for some ants or termites to eat. Flying dragons do not like to work for their food. They prefer to wait for the food to come to them. But as the dragon looks for the perfect spot on the tree trunk, he notices another, larger flying dragon on a branch. Flying dragons are territorial lizards. The other lizard lifts a bright-yellow flag-like skin flap under its chin. This is called a dewlap. Showing his dewlap is a warning to the smaller lizard. He can't stay without a fight. The smaller lizard lifts his dewlap, accepting the challenge. The larger lizard begins to bob his body back and forth to intimidate the smaller one.

The smaller lizard has second thoughts. He scampers up the tree, closely followed by his larger foe. The small lizard runs to the end of a branch. It's a dead end. Luckily, he has a means of escape. He leaps from the branch and spreads two flaps of skin to either side like a cape. These wings are supported by long ribs. They catch the air and the lizard glides to another tree. He uses his tail to steer, and his flat body makes him more aerodynamic. He can land on a tree 100 feet (30 m) away.[15] This new tree is unoccupied. The common flying dragon can settle in and wait for ants.

REAL-LIFE DRAGONS

The common flying dragon can't actually fly. It glides on the air like a hang glider, leaping from one tree to another. Its wings fold up against its sides until it needs them. This adaptation allows flying dragons to move more quickly than they could on the ground. The wings are mostly brown on the top and vary in color on the bottom. Females have yellow coloring on the undersides of their wings, and males have a bluish color there. The dewlap is yellow for males and blue-gray for females. The rest of the body is a mottled brown, allowing the lizard to camouflage itself against tree trunks. Common flying dragons grow to only about eight inches (20 cm) in length, with females slightly

FUN FACT

The common flying dragon is part of the genus *Draco*, which means "dragon" in Latin. There are more than 40 species in the genus *Draco*.[16]

larger than males.[17] A common flying dragon's tail accounts for more than half of its body length.

REPRODUCTION

Male flying dragons don't use their dewlaps only to intimidate other males. The lizards also show them off to attract females. A male dragon might extend his dewlap and wings, bob his body, and circle a female dragon to show his interest. If she isn't interested, she can raise her own dewlap to ward off the male.

Once a female dragon mates, she ventures to the ground to lay her eggs. She builds a nest by pushing her head into the ground and creating a hole. After laying her eggs, she covers the hole and pats down the dirt with her head. She will guard the eggs for a day before returning to the trees, leaving the eggs and hatchlings to fend for themselves.

COMMON FLYING DRAGON
Draco volans

SIZE
8 inches (20 cm)

WEIGHT
3–4 ounces (85–113 g)

RANGE
Southern India, Southeast Asia

HABITAT
Rain forests

DIET
Insects, especially ants and termites

LIFE SPAN
Approximately 8 years

The Eastern glass lizard may look like it's a snake, but it is a legless lizard.

A girl walks through the forest, her brother following with his camera. She stares intently at the ground, stopping every now and then to turn over a log or rustle through a pile of leaves with her snake hook. She is looking for reptiles to show on her YouTube channel. She is hoping to hit 1,000 subscribers by the end of the year.

She and her brother come to a grassy clearing when she sees something moving. She hurries over and picks up what looks like a snake. It thrashes and tries to roll out of her grip, releasing a smelly substance that makes her cough. But she keeps her gentle grip on the creature and excitedly holds it up to the camera. That's when she sees the creature blink at her. She tells her brother and her followers that this is not a snake at all—it's a legless lizard, specifically the Eastern glass lizard. She points out the features that distinguish legless lizards from snakes. The lizard has movable eyelids, which means it can blink, and visible earholes, which snakes do not have. It has a divot running down each side of its body called the lateral groove. She knows it's an Eastern glass lizard because it has no stripes below this groove.

She puts the lizard on the ground to show the camera how it moves. It darts away quickly. She tries to grab it again and its wriggling tail breaks off in her hand. The lizard burrows under a log and escapes, leaving its tail behind. The girl knows the lizard will be all right—it did this on purpose. The glass lizard gets its name from its fragile tail. Like many lizards, when threatened the Eastern glass lizard can break off its tail and escape. The piece left behind continues to twitch as a distraction for predators. The lizard's tail will grow back over time.

APPEARANCE

Of glass lizards, naturalist G. Earl Chance said, "It's hard to say which startles a person more, to find a snake that blinks or a lizard without legs."[18] Though they are sometimes called glass snakes, horn snakes, or joint snakes, Eastern glass lizards are not snakes but legless lizards. Other legless lizards include many skinks and most of the worm lizards. Scientists believe these lizards lost their limbs over time to better allow them to burrow.

Eastern glass lizards have long bodies composed mostly of their tails. The tail is nearly three times the length of the rest of the lizard. Eastern glass lizards can grow to more than

3.3 feet (1 m) in total length. Eastern glass lizards are usually greenish or brown, and some have black speckles that can look like stripes. Young lizards are usually khaki or tan with dark stripes down the sides of the body.

HABITAT AND BEHAVIOR

Eastern glass lizards can be found in flatwoods and sandy areas such as coastal dunes. Because they are burrowing lizards, they may be found under logs or in plowed fields. Unlike snakes, Eastern glass lizards do not have flexible jaws, meaning they eat smaller prey than snakes of a similar size. They eat mostly invertebrates such as insects, spiders, snails, and worms, but they can eat snakes and other glass lizards as well. They can also steal bird eggs from nests on the ground. While snakes would likely eat the eggs whole, Eastern glass lizards must crack the shells with their jaws and use their tongues to eat the insides.

FUN FACT

The Eastern glass lizard is the United States' longest native lizard.[19]

EASTERN GLASS LIZARD
Ophisaurus ventralis

SIZE
1.5–3.6 feet (0.5–1.1 m)

WEIGHT
0.7–1.3 pounds (0.3–0.6 kg) for all glass lizard species

RANGE
Southeastern United States

HABITAT
Flatwoods, wetlands, sandy areas

DIET
Invertebrates including insects, spiders, worms; reptiles including snakes, other glass lizards

LIFE SPAN
10–30 years in the wild

The Eastern long-necked turtle is adapted for spending long periods in the water.

An Eastern long-necked turtle swims along the bottom of an Australian swamp. She'll leave the water to lay her eggs in the summer. She might also leave to find a new home if food becomes scarce here. Otherwise she spends most of her time in the water, and her webbed toes help her swim.

The turtle settles onto the bottom of the swamp. It's time to find some food. Eastern long-necked turtles are ambush predators. They sit and wait for food to come to them. The turtle pulls her neck to the side along her shell. She isn't picky; she'll eat fish, tadpoles, plankton, or crustaceans. She'll even eat carrion. Soon a fish swims by. The turtle launches her head forward on her long neck, opening her mouth. Her neck and the floor of her mouth expand, sucking the unsuspecting fish right into her jaws.

This brings in water and other small invertebrates too. Then she closes her mouth and collapses her neck. This pushes out the water, but the food remains.

APPEARANCE AND HABITAT

Eastern long-necked turtle, common long-necked turtle, common snake-necked turtle, Eastern snake-necked turtle, and Australian snake-necked turtle are all common names for a single species: *Chelodina longicollis*. This freshwater turtle is native to southeastern Australia. No matter which name is used, they all focus on this creature's neck. The Eastern long-necked turtle is part of the suborder Pleurodira. Pleurodires are turtles that cannot pull their heads inside of their shells. Instead, a pleurodire tucks its neck and head to one side to protect itself. Pleurodires are found only in South America, Africa, and Australia. The Eastern long-neck is one of 14 long-necked turtles from Australia and the surrounding islands.

FUN FACT
Eastern long-necked turtles are seed dispersers. Seeds from water plants collect in the algae on their shells.

Eastern long-necked turtles are considered medium-sized turtles, and they average ten inches (25 cm) in length. The color of the carapace ranges from light brown to black, and it has a shallow groove in the center. The plastron is a lighter cream color with dark seams where the scutes come together, and the turtle's head and limbs are dark. Juveniles have additional orange coloring in spots on the plastron and stripes down the neck and jaw. Eastern long-necks

PLEURODIRES VS. CRYPTODIRES

PLEURODIRE

The Eastern long-necked turtle is a pleurodire. It pulls its long neck along the side of its shell for protection.

CRYPTODIRE

The red-eared slider is a cryptodire. It withdraws its head and neck straight back into its shell for protection.

can be found in rivers and streams, but they are more often found in swamps or wetlands that have slower-moving waters.

ON THE ROAD AGAIN

Eastern long-necked turtles are capable of incredible journeys when they need to find new habitats. A herpetologist named Terry Graham studied migration patterns of Eastern long-necked turtles in New South Wales, Australia, by attaching spools of thread to their shells. As the turtles moved, the thread left a path for Graham to follow. The turtles

moved in a straight line to a new feeding ground. The sun seemed to play an important role in the turtles' navigation, as the turtles rested on cloudy days. They also seemed to use the sense of smell and sometimes recognized landmarks on the way. Some Eastern long-necks have been recorded traveling as far as 3.2 miles (5.2 km).[20] If Eastern long-necked turtles can't move to another pond, they can bury themselves in the mud to hibernate for up to two and a half months. They can also hibernate underwater during colder weather.

EASTERN LONG-NECKED TURTLE
Chelodina longicollis

SIZE
10 inches (25 cm) long

WEIGHT
1.3 pounds (0.6 kg)

RANGE
Southeastern Australia

HABITAT
Swamps, wetlands; sometimes streams, rivers

DIET
Fish, tadpoles, plankton, invertebrates, crustaceans, carrion

LIFE SPAN
31–37 years on average in the wild and in captivity

Diego has helped to bring his species back from the brink of extinction.

It is a big day for Diego the giant tortoise. After more than 40 years as part of a captive breeding program, he is being released into the wild. Now 100 years old, Diego has lived a storied life. He was taken from his home, the island of Española in the Galápagos Islands, in the early 1900s. He was eventually brought to the San Diego Zoo in San Diego, California, in the 1930s. In the 1970s, researchers were worried about the population of giant tortoises on Española. They estimated that only 12 females and two males remained in the wild. Researchers brought them all to the Galápagos island of Santa Cruz to be part of a breeding program. The San Diego Zoo sent Diego to join the program in 1976. In his time in the breeding program, Diego fathered 40 percent of the nearly 2,000 Española tortoises born during that period.[21] He is credited with helping to save his species.

In 2020, the breeding program ended. It had done its job of restoring the Española tortoise. Diego was returned to Española, along with 14 other tortoises. They were quarantined to make sure they did not bring any plant seeds from Santa Cruz to Española in their digestive tracts. Then they were fitted with trackers and taken by boat to Española, which is uninhabited by people. The tortoises were strapped into harnesses and carried by humans onto the island before being released. After almost 100 years, Diego was finally home.

GALÁPAGOS GIANTS

Española is one of the 20 islands that make up the Galápagos Islands, which lie 563 miles (906 km) off the coast of Ecuador.[22] The islands are known for their biodiversity, and studying the unique animals there helped scientist Charles Darwin develop his theory of evolution. Originally the Galápagos giant tortoise was considered to be one species, *Chelonoidis nigra*, with 15 subspecies found on different islands. Now many scientists recognize the different tortoises as unique species. Only 11 of the species are still alive.

Española giant tortoises are among the species called saddleback tortoises. They are so named because Darwin noted the front of the carapace was "turned up like a Spanish saddle."[23] The species evolved to have a saddleback carapace that completely exposes the tortoise's neck. This exposure would make the tortoise extremely vulnerable. The species could only evolve in this way if it had no natural predators. A longer neck helps tortoises reach plants higher off the ground; it is also useful for asserting dominance over rival males. Saddleback Galápagos tortoises are usually smaller than tortoises with traditional domed shells, and they come from drier islands where food is less abundant.

THE GALÁPAGOS ISLANDS

Pacific Ocean

EQUATOR

San Salvador

Santa Cruz

Fernandina

Isabela

San Cristóbal

Floreana

Española

SOUTH AMERICA

ON THE BRINK OF EXTINCTION

Humans were responsible for driving these tortoises to the brink of extinction. Galápagos tortoises can survive for nearly a year without food or water. Because of this, sailors would take the tortoises as a source of food at sea. Human visitors to the

FUN FACT

Galápagos giant tortoises nap nearly 16 hours a day.[24] In hot weather they sometimes sleep partially submerged in mud.

Galápagos Islands also introduced invasive species. Rats and pigs fed on tortoise eggs, and goats destroyed local habitats, eating much of the tortoises' food.

The tortoises were saved through conservation efforts, such as breeding programs. On Española conservationists took another step, eliminating all goats from the island by 1978. Though the Española tortoise is still critically endangered, its population growth from 15 to 2,000 is a conservation success story.[25]

Young Galápagos tortoises at a nursery on the island of Santa Cruz

ESPAÑOLA GIANT TORTOISE
Chelonoidis hoodensis

SIZE
2.5–2.8 feet (77–86 cm) long

WEIGHT
Diego weighs 175 pounds (80 kg)

RANGE
Española in the Galápagos Islands

HABITAT
Dry shrublands, dry grasslands, forests

DIET
Cacti, especially prickly pear cacti; flowers, grasses, fruits

LIFE SPAN
More than 100 years in the wild and in captivity

The gharial looks similar to alligators and crocodiles, except for its much narrower snout.

It's a dark, warm night along the Chambal River in India. A 13-foot (4 m) gharial emerges from the river and drags herself up the sandy bank, beckoned by a chorus of squeaking sounds. The sounds are coming from her babies, still inside their eggs and buried in the sand. It's time for them to hatch, but they need their mother's help. She moves closer to the nest. Unlike other crocodilians, gharials cannot walk on land. Their legs can't support their weight. Instead, the mother stays on her belly and uses her legs to push herself along. When she finds the nest, she starts digging. Soon long, thin snouts begin poking through the eggshells. The gharials have hatched. They know by instinct to head to the river.

The baby gharials are only approximately seven inches (18 cm) long. They are far more vulnerable to predators than their enormous mother. Wild pigs, mongooses, and monitor lizards all prey on gharial eggs and hatchlings. A gharial will protect her babies for about six months until they can take care of themselves. She sometimes will watch another gharial's babies in addition to her own to give the other mother the opportunity to hunt. The other mother may return the favor. Male gharials will sometimes step in to protect the hatchlings as well. Researchers have observed younger males protecting babies they did not father. Researchers think this may be a younger male's way of showing female gharials he would be a good mate. The hatchlings ride around the river on the male's back, knowing they are safe from harm.

APPEARANCE AND BEHAVIOR

Gharials are crocodilians, belonging to the same order as alligators and crocodiles. But they are easily distinguished from other crocodilians by their unusual snouts. A gharial has a long and narrow snout filled with more than 100 teeth that interlock like a zipper.[26] These jaws are perfectly suited for catching fish. The thin jaws face little water resistance as they snap shut and trap struggling fish in their

A young gharial

razor-sharp teeth. Gharials are some of the largest crocodilians, and males can grow to nearly 21 feet (6.5 m). Females are smaller than males but can still grow to more than 13 feet (4 m). Adult gharials are usually brown or green with a yellow or white underbelly. Juveniles have dark bands that fade as they grow.

Besides size, there is another major difference between male and female gharials. Males have a growth on the end of the snout called a ghara. The ghara acts as a vocal resonator, allowing gharials to communicate by making a popping noise. A ghara can also help a male gharial attract a mate, as it is appealing to females.

CONSERVATION EFFORTS

Gharials are critically endangered, with fewer than 1,000 of them left in the wild.[27] While once found from Myanmar to Pakistan, they are now found only in a handful of rivers in India and Nepal. Human activity is the main reason for their decline. In addition to the indirect threat of habitat loss, gharials can become caught in fishing nets or lose their food sources to the fishing industry. Humans also poach gharials for their eggs, meat, skins, and gharas. The Indian government granted gharials full protection in the 1970s in an effort to reduce poaching. Groups such as the Gharial Multi-Task Force and the Gharial Ecology Project are working to save gharials. Conservation efforts include captive breeding programs and the careful study of remaining populations.

FUN FACT

Ghara is a Hindi word meaning "mud pot." The growth on a male gharial's snout resembles one of these pots, which is how the animal got its name.

The tip of a male gharial's snout

GHARIAL
Gavialis gangeticus

SIZE
Up to 21 feet (6.5 m) long

WEIGHT
350–399 pounds (159–181 kg)

RANGE
Northern India, Nepal

HABITAT
Freshwater rivers

DIET
Fish; juveniles will also eat frogs, insects, crustaceans

LIFE SPAN
40–60 years on average in the wild

Gila monsters leave their dens to take advantage of the sun's heat.

A Gila monster comes out of its burrow in Saguaro National Park in Arizona. Gila monsters spend most of their lives underground, emerging to feed and bask in the sun. This Gila monster has not eaten in months, and it is hungry. Gila monsters are slow movers compared to other lizards. They usually go after easy-to-capture prey such as reptile eggs, baby mammals, or birds, crushing the prey with their strong jaws. But the Gila monster's favorite food is eggs. It begins the hunt, smelling the air by flicking its dark, forked tongue in and out of its mouth. It can find eggs buried nearly six inches (15 cm) under the ground.[28] It is not afraid to climb trees or cacti in search of bird eggs, and it can even track eggs that have rolled away.

Eventually, its sense of smell leads it to a clutch of tortoise eggs. It cracks the shell of an egg and feasts on the yolk inside. Because it feeds so rarely, it can eat up to 35 percent of its body weight in a single feeding.[29] The Gila monster's short, round tail serves as a fat reserve. It can live off the fat stored in its tail between feedings. Once it has eaten its fill, it returns to its underground haven. It will be several months before the Gila monster needs to feed again.

DESERT DWELLER

Gila monsters are native to the deserts of the southwestern United States and northwestern Mexico. They grow up to two feet (61 cm) long. Though they are found in deserts, they prefer areas with some moisture, such as canyons with streams. This is because a Gila monster easily loses moisture through its skin.

The Gila monster is one of a few species in the beaded lizard family, so named for the tiny bumps all over these lizards' skin. These bumps are known as osteoderms. Each one is an individual scale with a small bead of protective bone inside it. Gila monsters are black with pink, yellow, or salmon spotted patterns.

VENOMOUS LIZARD

The Gila monster's coloring also serves as a warning to potential predators. Gila monsters are one of only a handful of venomous lizard species in the world. Gila monsters do not use venom for hunting but for defense. Unlike venomous snakes, Gila monsters do not have fangs. Rather than deliver venom with a single strike, they must gnaw on their targets to release the venom created in their salivary glands. The bite is painful, but no recorded human deaths have occurred as a result of a Gila monster bite. US Geological

FUN FACT

A synthetic version of a hormone found in Gila monster venom has been used to treat diabetes in humans.

Survey ecologist Cecil Schwalbe described a Gila monster bite, saying, "It was one of the most painful experiences I've ever had. My finger felt like it was on fire, and this wave of fire kept moving up my arm. I got nauseous, I had difficulty breathing . . . I had just a marvelous systemic reaction to the poison in this creature."[30]

GILA MONSTER
Heloderma suspectum

SIZE
1.7–2 feet (52–61 cm)

WEIGHT
4–5 pounds (1.8–2.3 kg) or more

RANGE
Southwestern United States, northwestern Mexico

HABITAT
Arid areas including deserts, canyons and arroyos, mountain slopes

DIET
Small mammals, lizards, birds; eggs of birds, reptiles

LIFE SPAN
Up to 20 years in the wild

Only the top half of the anaconda's head is exposed as it waits for prey to come near.

A green anaconda is motionless in the small stream. Her eyes and nostrils are on the top of her head, allowing her to keep the rest of her enormous body completely submerged. She is more than 20 feet (6 m) long and weighs more than 300 pounds (136 kg). Her bulk slows her down on land, but she can move easily in the water. She is lying in wait for prey.

Soon a family of capybaras approaches the water. The world's largest rodents, capybaras spend a good portion of their time near water to feed on aquatic plants. The anaconda moves silently through the water toward an adult in the group. The capybara is more than four feet (1.2 m) long and weighs 100 pounds (45 kg), but it's no match for the anaconda. The anaconda attacks, latching her jaws onto the capybara and wrapping her enormous body around the rodent.

Multiple rows of backward-facing teeth lock the snake's jaws in place, but it is not the bite that kills. Anacondas are constrictors, using their long bodies and strong muscles to slowly squeeze prey to death. Constricting stops the flow of blood to the prey's heart as well as its ability to breathe. When the capybara is dead, the anaconda eats it whole, starting with the head. The anaconda's rows of teeth move independently to pull the capybara into its jaws, which stretch wide to accommodate

FUN FACT

Like other large snakes, the anaconda has evolved to push its windpipe out from inside its throat. This lets the snake breathe while consuming large prey.

A green anaconda after swallowing a capybara

its prey. It can take up to eight hours for the anaconda to finish its meal. But when it is finished, it won't need to eat again for months.

HEAVYWEIGHT SNAKE

The green anaconda is the heaviest snake in the world. Though reticulated pythons can grow longer, green anacondas can be nearly twice as heavy. Reports vary on exactly how large anacondas can be. People who see anacondas in the wild might overestimate the snake's length due to fear, and it can be difficult to get anacondas in captivity to fully stretch out in order to measure them. How recently an anaconda has eaten can also affect how large it looks. Weight has to be estimated as well. But *National Geographic* reports that green anacondas can grow to nearly 30 feet (9 m) and weigh up to 550 pounds (250 kg).

The green anaconda can grow to incredible sizes.

The green anaconda takes its name from the olive-green color of its back. Black blotches and spots on the snake's body allow it to camouflage among plants in the water. Females are much larger than males. Females reach an average length of 20 feet (6 m) while males reach an average of 10 feet (3 m). Female anacondas are known to eat males, especially after mating.

LIVE BIRTH

Unlike many snakes, anacondas do not lay eggs. The mother anaconda carries her eggs inside her body and the babies hatch inside. She then gives birth to live young. Green anacondas give birth to 20 to 40 offspring at a time on average, but they can birth as many as 80 offspring. The eggs incubate inside the mother for seven months, and she does not eat during this time. After giving birth, a female anaconda may eat undeveloped eggs or babies who did not survive in order to regain her strength. Baby anacondas, approximately two feet (61 cm) long at birth, are fully independent and do not rely on the mother's care.[31]

GREEN ANACONDA
Eunectes murinus

SIZE
Males average 10 feet (3 m); females average 20 feet (6 m)

WEIGHT
Up to 550 pounds (250 kg)

RANGE
South America, especially Colombia, Brazil, Venezuela

HABITAT
Tropical savannas, rain forests, grasslands; marshes, swamps, slow-moving streams

DIET
Anything it can overpower, including caimans, capybaras, deer, jaguars

LIFE SPAN
10 years on average in the wild; more than 30 years in captivity

GREEN SEA TURTLE

Baby green sea turtles must make a harrowing journey from the beach to the sea.

On a tropical beach near the Great Barrier Reef, the sand is beginning to shift. A tiny green sea turtle hatchling emerges. Soon others join it. The hatchlings each weigh less than one ounce (28 g) and are only two inches (5 cm) long.[32] There are more than 100 eggs buried beneath the sand.[33] Two months ago, the turtles' mother emerged from the sea to lay her eggs on the beach. She dug a nest with her legs, laid her eggs, then covered the nest and returned to the ocean. The hatchlings are now on their own.

The green turtle hatchlings know they must go to the ocean, but a gauntlet of obstacles lies ahead of them. Birds circle overhead, hoping to snatch up a juvenile turtle as a snack. Crabs on the beach also pose a threat. The turtles begin to scurry across the sand. There is strength in numbers as they make their way toward the water, but some are snatched away by predators. Even the ones who make it to the water's edge aren't home free. Some hatchlings drown in the pounding waves beating upon the shore. Those that do make it to the open sea must contend with predators there. Only about one in 1,000 green sea turtle hatchlings will make it to adulthood.[34]

BEING GREEN

Green sea turtles are named for their greenish skins and the green-colored fat inside their bodies. The turtles' shells are olive or brown. Hatchlings are born black and gradually change color as they reach maturity, which happens between ages 27 and 50. Sea turtle shells do not have a gap inside for the turtle's head and limbs. This shape is streamlined, allowing the turtles to move more easily through the water. Sea turtles use their longer front legs to propel themselves forward. The shorter back legs are used to steer. Green turtles are among the largest species of sea turtles. Adults grow to have a carapace length of up to four feet (1.2 m) and can weigh more than 400 pounds (181 kg).

Green turtles are an endangered species. Adult green turtles have few natural predators at sea besides sharks. It is largely human action that threatens them, including accidental catching in fishing nets and illegal poaching of sea turtle meat and eggs. Pollution can have a devastating effect on sea turtle habitats.

FUN FACT

Sea turtle hatchlings use light on the horizon as a guide toward the ocean. Artificial light can make them head toward cars and predators.

MIGRATION AND MAGNETISM

Once a female green sea turtle reaches maturity, she will return to the beach where she was born to lay her eggs. Some populations of green sea turtles stay relatively close to their breeding grounds to feed, but others go on journeys of thousands of miles. Sea turtles are able to sense Earth's magnetic field. This allows them to navigate back to the beaches where they were born. As a turtle gets closer, it may use sensory cues such as smell to locate its precise destination. Females can lay anywhere from 75 to 200 eggs in a clutch and can lay up to nine clutches per nesting season, though the average is three. They breed every two to four years.

A green sea turtle lays its eggs.

GREEN SEA TURTLE
Chelonia mydas

SIZE
Carapace 3.3–4 feet (1–1.2 m) long

WEIGHT
331–441 pounds (150–200 kg)

RANGE
Atlantic Ocean, Pacific Ocean, Mediterranean Sea, Indian Ocean

HABITAT
Tropical and subtropical oceans

DIET
Seagrasses, other aquatic plants; juveniles also eat invertebrates

LIFE SPAN
80 years or more in the wild

KING COBRA

The widened neck hood is a distinctive feature of the king cobra.

A yellow rat snake slithers through a forest in southern Asia. It's on the hunt for a rat to eat. But it does not realize the hunter is about to become the hunted. A king cobra looks down from a tree. The cobra can spot prey 300 feet (90 m) away, and the rat snake has caught its eye.[35] The king cobra's genus, *Ophiophagus*, means "snake eater." The reason for this name is about to become clear.

The cobra slowly advances on the rat snake. The rat snake tries to flee, but it's too late. The cobra strikes from more than three feet (91 cm) away. It has something the rat snake does not: venom. The venom flows from the cobra's sharp, hollow fangs into the rat snake's body. The cobra releases enough venom in one bite to kill an elephant. The rat snake tries to fight back, but it stands no chance. The venom attacks its nervous system, paralyzing the rat snake. Once the rat snake is immobilized, the king cobra swallows it whole. Backward-facing teeth help pull the rat snake inside the cobra's jaws. The cobra's venom starts breaking the snake down, aiding the digestive process.

VENOMOUS BITE

King cobras are the longest venomous snakes on Earth, growing up to 18 feet (5.5 m) long.[36] They are among the most venomous snakes on earth. This is due not to the potency of the venom itself but how much of it can be delivered in a single bite—enough to kill

20 people.[37] Cobra venom is a neurotoxin, meaning it affects the nervous system. It acts quickly to paralyze victims. King cobras deliver venom through their fangs. These fangs are fixed and do not move, which means the fangs have to be short enough for cobras to close their jaws. Fangs are typically only 0.3 to 0.4 inches (0.8–1 cm) long.[38]

FUN FACT

Though king cobras are often used in snake charming acts, they cannot hear music. Instead, they are reacting to the swaying pipe.

A king cobra can lift one-third of its body off the ground when it goes into a defensive posture. It may flare out its neck hood and give a low hiss. It can continue to move even in this position. But despite their fearsome reputations, king cobras would rather flee than fight. They rarely attack humans unless provoked. One exception is a female cobra guarding her nest. The mother cobra is highly protective of her eggs, creating a nest for them and guarding them fiercely. During this time, cobras may attack humans unprovoked. Still, king cobras only kill approximately five people per year across their entire range.[39]

APPEARANCE AND DIET

King cobras are typically black, green, yellow, or brown. They have light-yellow or cream-colored throats and may have white or yellowish bands across the body. Baby king cobras are black with distinct bands that can fade over time. The cobra's famous hood is created by ribs on the neck. It can stretch out these bones to appear larger and more threatening to adversaries.

A king cobra's main source of food is other snakes. Common species eaten by king cobras include pythons and Asian rat snakes. However, these cobras may also eat eggs, lizards, and small mammals.

KING COBRA
Ophiophagus hannah

SIZE
Up to 18 feet (5.5 m) long

WEIGHT
Up to 20 pounds (9 kg)

RANGE
Northern India, southern China, Malay Peninsula, Indonesia, the Philippines

HABITAT
Forests, mangrove swamps, bamboo thickets

DIET
Mostly other snakes; also eggs, lizards, small mammals

LIFE SPAN
20 years on average in the wild

Like many reptiles, Komodo dragons have forked tongues.

In the grassy savanna of Komodo National Park in Indonesia, a predator lies in wait. It is a Komodo dragon, named for one of the islands on which these enormous lizards are found. This one is stalking a nearby water buffalo, waiting for a chance to strike. The buffalo is grazing, oblivious to the dragon's presence. Suddenly, the dragon lunges. It latches its powerful jaws onto the buffalo's leg. The buffalo escapes, but this is still a victory for the dragon. Its bite leaves bloody wounds. Now the dragon just has to wait.

The Komodo dragon stalks its prey, using its forked tongue to track the buffalo's scent. The dragon can track the buffalo's location from more than six miles (9.7 km) away with the right wind conditions. The buffalo is growing weaker as it loses blood. The buffalo's blood pressure drops. It eventually collapses into a watering hole. The bacteria in the unclean water will almost certainly infect the wound. There is no escape now. The Komodo dragon finds the buffalo and begins to feast.

DIET AND BEHAVIOR

Komodo dragons are the largest lizards in the world, reaching lengths of up to ten feet (3 m) and weighing more than 300 pounds (136 kg). A Komodo dragon's bulk slows it down. Its top speed is only approximately

12 miles per hour (19 kmh), making it difficult for a dragon to catch quick-footed prey, such as deer.[40] Komodo dragons instead rely on their venom to do the hard work, leisurely following their prey and eating it after it has died. One bite is all it takes to bring prey down.

Multiple dragons will often come together to feast on larger prey. They will eat nearly every part of the animal, leaving little waste.

FUN FACT

Komodo dragons have a bite force of 60 pounds per square inch (414 kPa).[41]

For decades, scientists believed that bacteria, not venom, was the Komodo dragon's secret weapon. A scientist observing Komodo dragons noted that large prey often developed infections after being bitten by the dragons. He suggested that Komodo dragons have toxic bacteria in their saliva, and the idea stuck. It was not until 2009 that researchers discovered that Komodo dragons have venom glands, and that the infections in prey are likely caused by contaminated water.

REPRODUCTION AND EARLY LIFE

When a female Komodo dragon is ready to mate, she gives off a scent in her feces that males can follow. But if males are scarce, female Komodo dragons can reproduce on their own through parthenogenesis. Female Komodo dragons possess both male and female sex chromosomes, meaning they can fertilize their own eggs and give birth without the presence of a male. The resulting offspring are all male, which means parthenogenesis is not the perfect solution for continuing the species. But it is still a valuable evolutionary trait.

Juvenile Komodo dragons are too small to be the fearsome predators that the adults are. In fact, juvenile dragons face predation from adults of their own species. A young dragon will spend the first eight months of its life living in the trees, where the adults can't reach. Full-grown Komodo dragons are too heavy to climb trees effectively. A juvenile will feed on invertebrates, eggs, small reptiles, and small mammals as it grows. At eight months it will move to a more terrestrial life, as it will have grown too large to live in the trees.

A young Komodo dragon climbs a tree to escape its adult counterparts.

KOMODO DRAGON
Varanus komodoensis

SIZE
Up to 10 feet (3 m)

WEIGHT
Can weigh more than 300 pounds (136 kg)

RANGE
Indonesia's Lesser Sunda Islands

HABITAT
Tropical savannas and forests

DIET
Carrion, juvenile Komodo dragons, large prey such as deer, boar, goats, water buffalo

LIFE SPAN
Approximately 50 years in the wild

A painted turtle hatchling

I t is late autumn in North America. A dozen painted turtle hatchlings have emerged from their leathery eggshells. Their mother laid her eggs in a nest near the water, digging a hole and creating a plug that left open air between the eggs and the soil. The eggs are less than six inches (15 cm) below the surface.[42] Most turtles would try to emerge from the nest after hatching. But winter is coming, and these hatchlings stay put. They pull their heads and limbs into their shells and prepare to hibernate.

The hatchlings can survive temperatures as low as 14 degrees Fahrenheit (–10°C). Ice crystals form on their bodies and in the body fluids outside their cells. This is a delicate time; if ice crystals form inside the hatchlings' cells, they may not survive.

But painted turtles are resilient. They are capable of tolerating cold temperatures, preventing the formation of ice crystals within their cells, and withstanding ice crystals that do form outside their cells and on their exteriors. Many other turtle species cannot survive such freezing events.

The turtle hatchlings can stay frozen for six months. When spring arrives, the ice melts and the turtles begin to move again. They dig their way out of the nest. They have avoided the food scarcity of the colder months and are ready to thrive in their new environments.

APPEARANCE AND BEHAVIOR

Painted turtles are some of the most wide-ranging turtles in North America, inhabiting southern Canada and much of the United States. They are also some of the most thoroughly researched freshwater turtles in the world. The painted turtle gets its name from its brightly colored markings. These markings are different in the four subspecies. Western painted turtles are the most brilliantly colored. This subspecies boasts a red plastron with yellow and black markings. The other three subspecies have plain yellow plastrons, but the carapaces vary. In general, the carapaces have red and yellow markings on a background of black or greenish brown. The southern painted turtle, sometimes considered its own species, has a red stripe down its carapace. Eastern and midland painted turtles can be differentiated by the pattern of their scutes. All painted turtles have red colorings on the underside of the carapace. The head and limbs are black with yellow stripes.

Painted turtles spend most of their time in the water, but they are often seen basking in the sun. They may bask on logs, rocks, or other objects. This helps warm the body and also

Painted turtles sometimes stack on top of one another while basking in the sun.

kills leeches and other parasites. Sometimes as many as 50 turtles will bask on the same log, some of them stacked on top of one another.[43]

HIBERNATION

Painted turtle hatchlings remain in their nests to get through the cold winter months. But adults take a slightly different approach. They bury themselves in mud to insulate against the cold. They can survive the winter under the ice of a frozen pond. A hibernating painted turtle slows down its metabolism; its heart may beat once every five to ten minutes. This slows the production of lactic acid, a chemical normally expelled by breathing that can become toxic at elevated levels. In addition to slowing the rate at which lactic acid is produced, the turtles can absorb the acid into their shells. Minerals found in the shells act as a buffer to keep lactic acid from becoming toxic. As the painted turtle thaws and begins to breathe again, it releases the stored lactic acid and expels it through breathing.

FUN FACT

A painted turtle shows that it is ready to mate by stroking another turtle's face with its claws.

PAINTED TURTLE
Chrysemys picta

SIZE
Carapace 3.5–9.8 inches (9–25 cm) long

WEIGHT
13.1 ounces (372 g) on average

RANGE
Southern Canada and most of the United States

HABITAT
Shallow freshwater habitats with thick mud

DIET
Carrion, crustaceans, fish, aquatic plants

LIFE SPAN
Up to 61 years in the wild

Saltwater crocodiles are dominant predators in their ecosystems.

On the banks of a river in Papua New Guinea, love is in the air. A female saltwater crocodile has just chased off a younger female from her territory, snapping her jaws and chasing the challenger out of the water. A nearby male saw this, and he is impressed. He lumbers into the water and swims toward the female. She takes the lead, showing her interest by rubbing his snout and blowing bubbles against his jaw. The two mate, then part ways.

Now that she has mated, she can lay her eggs. Saltwater crocodiles can lay up to 90 eggs in a single clutch, though laying 40 to 60 eggs is more common. The crocodile creates a mounded nest out of mud and plant matter. It's the wet season, so the nest needs to be elevated to keep from flooding. As with many turtles, lizards, and crocodiles, the temperature of the nest will determine whether the babies are male or female. She buries her eggs, staying by the nest to guard them. She will attack anything that comes too close.

APPEARANCE AND BEHAVIOR

Saltwater crocodiles are the largest living reptiles on Earth. Males can grow up to 23 feet (7 m) long, though 17-foot (5 m) crocs are more common. Females are smaller than males, usually not growing past 9.8 feet (3 m). Juvenile saltwater crocodiles are pale yellow with black spots and stripes. As the crocodiles age, they become darker, settling into a gray or light tan color with a yellow or white belly. Adults will retain stripes on their sides.

As the name implies, saltwater crocodiles often live in saltwater habitats, but they can also live in fresh water. They are excellent swimmers and can be found far out at sea. They are common in northern Australia, Southeast Asia, and eastern India. Breeding and raising young take place in freshwater rivers. As juveniles age, males fight for dominance in the rivers. Males who can't establish a territory in the river must swim out to sea in search of a new river system.

FEARSOME HUNTERS, LOVING MOTHERS

Unlike many reptiles, which do not interact with their offspring after laying eggs, crocodilians care for their offspring. In addition to fiercely guarding the nest, a saltwater crocodile mother will help dig out her hatchlings after they hatch. The hatchlings make a chirping noise to alert their mother. She will then carry them into the water in her mouth. The baby crocodiles will stay with their mother until they can swim and hunt on their own.

FUN FACT

Saltwater crocodiles are called "salties" in Australia. They are sometimes also called "Indo-Pacific crocodiles" or simply "crocs."

Saltwater crocodiles are fearsome predators. They are ambush predators, lying in wait with all but their eyes and nostrils submerged. A saltwater crocodile will lunge out of the water to attack prey, using its powerful jaws and sharp teeth to pull prey down into the water. Saltwater crocodiles can take down buffalo and wild boars, as well as monkeys, turtles, snakes, and crabs. Juvenile crocodiles go after smaller prey such as crustaceans, amphibians, insects, and fish. The saltwater crocodile has a valve in its throat that it can close to keep from drowning when opening its mouth underwater.

A baby saltwater crocodile emerges from its egg.

SALTWATER CROCODILE
Crocodylus porosus

SIZE
Males up to 23 feet (7 m); females up to 9.8 feet (3 m)

WEIGHT
1,000 pounds (450 kg) on average; up to 2,200 pounds (1,000 kg)

RANGE
Northern Australia, Southeast Asia, eastern India

HABITAT
Freshwater rivers, coastal waters

DIET
Buffalo, boars, monkeys, birds, snakes, turtles, crabs

LIFE SPAN
70 years on average in the wild

A spiny softshell turtle basks on a rock.

Near Lake Champlain in northern Vermont, researchers at the ECHO Lake Aquarium and Science Center are working to protect local turtles. Spiny softshell turtles are common throughout the United States, but their population in this area is threatened. While adults have few natural predators, spiny softshell turtle eggs face predation from raccoons and skunks, and hatchlings can be eaten by birds, fish, and raccoons. Workers from the Vermont Fish and Wildlife service bring eggs and baby turtles from the beach to the ECHO center. There, workers will care for the hatchlings until they are big enough to have a better chance of surviving in the wild. Spiny softshell turtle eggs are the size of a quarter, and the hatchlings are approximately the size of a plastic milk cap. Only 2 percent of the eggs a female lays in her life will survive to produce breeding adults.[44] As the turtles grow larger, fewer things will be able to eat them.

While at the center, the turtles are used to educate the public about their importance to the environment. Though adults have no natural predators, they face threats from humans. This comes from habitat loss due to human development, as well as accidental killing by human boaters. In addition, people poach spiny softshell turtles for human consumption. Since adult females are larger, they are more likely to be poached than males; this affects population levels. When people learn about the turtles, they can take steps to help them.

APPEARANCE

The spiny softshell turtle has a soft, flat, leathery shell with no scutes. The edges of the shell can bend. This streamlined shape helps

The eggs of a spiny softshell turtle

make the spiny softshell an excellent swimmer. The carapace has small spines along the edges. Whether the spines are on the front, back, or all around the shell depends on the subspecies of spiny softshell. Spiny softshells usually have olive or tan shells. Males often have distinct spots on their shells while females are more mottled. The turtles have spotted or striped webbed feet with claws, and they have yellow-and-black stripes on their heads.

Perhaps the most notable feature of the spiny softshell turtle is its long nose. The turtle's long neck and tubular, snorkel-like nose allow it to breathe air while keeping the rest of its body submerged. With their mouths closed, aquatic turtles can expand and contract their throats to draw air into the lungs. Underwater, they use the same mechanism to draw water into the mouth—a special flap at the back of the mouth keeps water out of the lungs, which would cause drowning—and the lining of the mouth absorbs oxygen from the water. They can also absorb oxygen through the skin. A spiny softshell can obtain 22 percent to 50 percent of its oxygen from the water.[45]

FUN FACT

Spiny softshell turtles bury themselves on the bottoms of streams for the winter. They extend their necks into the water to take in oxygen.

BEHAVIOR AND DIET

Spiny softshells are most active during the day. They spend the majority of their time in the water, but they will bask in the sun on riverbanks and logs. They are effective at this and can heat their bodies twice as fast as they cool down. Spiny softshells are speedy swimmers. When threatened, they will dive in the water and bury themselves in the sand or mud on the bottom. They prefer freshwater habitats with little vegetation and sandy bottoms, along with beaches where they can lay their eggs.

These turtles are carnivorous, feeding on crustaceans, insects, and occasionally fish. They prefer to feed on the bottom of a body of water, ambushing prey as it approaches. They play important roles in keeping populations of their prey in check.

SPINY SOFTSHELL TURTLE
Apalone spinifera

SIZE
Carapace 9.5–18.9 inches (24–48 cm) for females; 4.7–9.5 inches (12–24 cm) for males

WEIGHT
25.8 pounds (11.7 kg) maximum

RANGE
Native to parts of southern Canada, midwestern and central United States, northern Mexico; introduced to eastern and southwestern United States

HABITAT
Freshwater lakes, marshes, rivers, bays of the Great Lakes; areas with little vegetation and sandy or muddy bottoms and riverbanks

DIET
Insects, crustaceans, occasionally fish

LIFE SPAN
50 years in the wild

Tokay geckos, like other gecko species, can cling to vertical walls.

In a small village in northern Thailand, a woman has an unusual roommate. A tokay gecko clings to the wall behind her mirror above the sink. Though these creatures are commonly sold as pets, this one is completely wild. The woman and the gecko have a mutually beneficial relationship. The gecko eats unwanted insects and pests in the home. In return, the woman gives the gecko a safe place to lay her eggs, as well as shelter from poachers.

In a nearby village, wild tokay geckos have all but disappeared. Poachers have taken all of the geckos they could find. Some are sold as pets. But the majority are killed, dried on sticks, and exported to China, Hong Kong, Taiwan, Vietnam, and elsewhere. The dried geckos are used in alternative medicines said to treat cancer, diabetes, and HIV/AIDS, though there is no proof of such treatments being effective. Poachers can earn 200 baht, equal to about six or seven US dollars, for a large gecko.[46] By allowing the gecko to stay in her home, this woman keeps it safe from those who might harm it.

APPEARANCE AND BEHAVIOR

Tokay geckos are among the largest living species of gecko, growing as

long as 16 inches (40 cm). They have bumpy, velvety skin that is grayish-blue with colored spots. In red-spotted tokays, the spots can be red, light yellow, or anywhere in between. Black-spotted tokays are another variety. A tokay can change its skin color slightly, lightening or darkening it to better camouflage itself against its environment. Males are slightly bigger than females and more brightly colored. The tokay's eyes are large with vertical pupils. Like many lizards, it has the remnants of a third eye on the top of its head. This third eye does not have vision in the way the fully developed eyes do, but it is sensitive to light. The gecko's ears are visible as small holes on either side of the head.

FUN FACT

Tokay geckos are named for the sound they make, which many people say sounds like "to-kay."

Tokays are known for their aggression and have fearsome bites. The tokay gecko's jaws are lined with tiny, sharp teeth that it will use to defend itself. Another defense mechanism is the ability to shed its tail. If a tokay gecko is caught by the tail, it can detach the tail and run away. The tail will continue twitching to distract the predator. The gecko's tail will eventually grow back, but the new one is usually shorter than the original.

CLIMBING TO NEW HEIGHTS

Along with many other gecko species, tokay geckos are capable of climbing smooth and vertical surfaces, and they can even cling upside down to horizontal surfaces. They are able to do this because of millions of tiny, hair-like structures on their toes called setae. Setae

TOKAY GECKO
Gekko gecko

SIZE
Males 13–16 inches (35–40 cm); females 8–12 inches (20–30 cm)

WEIGHT
5–14 ounces (142–397 g)

RANGE
Native to Southeast and East Asia, including China, Thailand, Indonesia, the Philippines; introduced in Hawaii, Florida, some Caribbean islands, Madagascar

HABITAT
Tropical rain forests

DIET
Mostly invertebrates, including grasshoppers, cockroaches, mosquitoes, spiders, moths; may also eat mice, rats, small snakes

LIFE SPAN
Around 10 years in captivity; estimated less in the wild

are made up of triangle-shaped projections called spatulae that are less than a thousandth of a millimeter wide. One gecko has billions of spatulae on its four feet. The spatulae each form a weak atomic bond with the surface, allowing the gecko to cling to surfaces other creatures could not. A tokay gecko is capable of holding onto a vertical surface with a single toe.

The tuatara is sometimes called a "living fossil" because it looks so similar to its ancestors from millions of years ago.

Deep in the forests of New Zealand, a tuatara is getting ready to hatch. Buried in the soil is a clutch of around a dozen eggs. They have been incubating for 16 months—the longest incubation period of any reptile.[47] Suddenly a tiny puncture appears in the shell of an egg. Thick liquid oozes out. The baby tuatara uses an egg tooth, a small spike on its nose, to crack its shell. Soon its siblings do the same. The hatchlings dig their way out of the nest. It's time to hunt.

But hunting proves tricky. Each hatchling is approximately 3.9 inches (10 cm) long. They are tiny in a world of giant predators. Tuataras mainly eat insects, but here in

New Zealand, insects such as the weta, a cricket-like insect the size of a gerbil, are hardly easy prey. A tuatara hatchling faces danger even from its own kind. Adult tuataras have no qualms about cannibalizing the young. When a young tuatara finds itself face-to-face with an adult, it holds perfectly still. As soon as a passing cockroach steals the adult's attention, the hatchling flees. Since adult tuataras are active at night, it will be safest for the hatchling to hunt during the day, when the adults are resting.

PREHISTORIC PREDATORS

At first glance tuataras may look like lizards, but they are only distantly related. The tuatara is the last remaining species of the order Rhynchocephalia, which dates back to the Triassic Period. Its closest relatives went extinct approximately 60 million years ago.[48] A distinct arrangement of the bones of the skull distinguishes the tuatara from lizards. The tuatara is found only on

approximately 30 islands throughout New Zealand.[49] While scientists once recognized two species, most now agree that all tuataras belong to the same species.

Tuataras are the largest reptiles in New Zealand, reaching up to two feet (61 cm) long. They are olive-green, gray, or orangish-red, and they can change color over a lifetime. The name *tuatara* comes from the Maori word for "peaks on the back." The reptile is so named for the line of spikes starting at the neck and stretching down the back. The male's spikes are larger than the female's, and males are typically larger in general. Unlike many animals, a tuatara's teeth are not grown in sockets but are firmly connected directly to the jaw. This means the teeth cannot be replaced if lost or broken, so adult tuataras often must resort to softer food as their teeth wear down. Two rows of teeth on the top jaw and one on the bottom interlock, easily cutting through prey.

UNDER THREAT

Tuataras in New Zealand once numbered in the millions. The arrival of Polynesians and the kiore, or Polynesian rat, approximately 1,000 years ago was a big trial for the tuatara. The kiore preyed on tuatara eggs and hatchlings. When European settlers arrived with rats on their ships, these

FUN FACT

The New Zealand government has fully protected tuataras by law since 1895.

rats also preyed on tuataras and competed for resources. The tuatara's numbers dropped. Removing rats and other rodents from the islands is one way conservationists are helping the tuatara. Another is through breeding programs. Hatchlings are raised until they are big enough to have a better chance of survival. Then they are released into the wild. A breeding program on Little Barrier Island began with eight tuataras and resulted in a population of around 300.[50]

TUATARA
Sphenodon punctatus

SIZE
1.3–2 feet (40–61 cm)

WEIGHT
1.1–2.2 pounds (0.5–1 kg)

RANGE
New Zealand

HABITAT
Forests

DIET
Bird eggs, small birds, frogs, lizards, young tuataras, invertebrates such as earthworms, snails, wetas

LIFE SPAN
60 years on average

VEILED CHAMELEON

Veiled chameleons use their feet and tails to tightly grip branches as they move.

A veiled chameleon slowly moves along a tree branch in Yemen. He lifts two feet, bobs slowly back and forth, then finally takes a step. The chameleon does this to mimic the movement of leaves, camouflaging himself in the trees. He is on the hunt for prey, but what he finds instead is another male encroaching on his territory. Veiled chameleons are aggressive and territorial; he will not stand for this invasion. The chameleon begins to change color. Light greens turn to vivid orange, red, and white. He opens his mouth, hissing and lunging at the intruder. The intruder matches this vivid coloring. The two grapple, hissing and snapping at one another. Finally the intruder relents, darkening his colors as a sign of surrender. He leaves the tree. The victorious chameleon continues his hunt.

MASTER OF DISGUISE

There are more than 170 different chameleon species.[51] Veiled chameleons are found natively only in Yemen and Saudi Arabia, though they have become invasive in other areas due to their popularity as pets. The veiled chameleon is named for the bony protrusion on the top of its head, called a casque. Males and females both have casques, though males' are larger. The casque helps steer water droplets into the chameleon's mouth, which is important in its dry habitat.

Contrary to popular belief, chameleons do not change color to blend in with their backgrounds. The characteristic back-and-forth movement of chameleons is far more important to their camouflage. Instead, chameleons change color to communicate with other chameleons. A resting male veiled chameleon is usually light green with yellow, blue, and brown accents. Females are a lighter green with white markings. Males will display vibrant colors when challenging other males or when courting females.

A male participating in a courtship display presents himself with a coiled tail and stiff legs, turning sideways to appear larger. He might bob his head and approach a female slowly. This caution is warranted—females are known to bite. If a female has already mated and is not interested, she will become more darkly colored, sporting turquoise and orange

FUN FACT

Veiled chameleons are one of the most popular reptile species to own as pets.

spots. Crystals and pigments in the cells of the chameleon's skin are what give it this ability. Chameleons change the spacing between the crystals and the concentrations of pigments under the cells, which changes the wavelength of light reflected off the chameleons' skin.

LIFE IN THE TREES

Chameleons are especially suited for life lived primarily in the trees. Each of a chameleon's feet is made of two pads, one with two toes and the other with three. These pads grip branches tightly. A chameleon's legs are situated directly under its body, unlike with other lizards, which have legs extending out to the sides. This allows the chameleon to better balance on branches. It also makes

use of its prehensile tail, which can grip branches as if it were another limb.

Chameleons have conical eyes that can rotate independently of one another. These eyes give chameleons a complete view around their bodies, except for directly above or below. The eyes can also zoom in like camera lenses. A chameleon uses its sticky tongue to catch insects. It can launch its tongue more than two body lengths from its mouth. This allows it to surprise its prey, catching it from a considerable distance away.

VEILED CHAMELEON
Chamaeleo calyptratus

SIZE
Males 1.4–2 feet (43–61 cm); females 0.8–1.2 feet (24–37 cm)

WEIGHT
3–6 ounces (85–170 g)

RANGE
Native to Saudi Arabia, Yemen; invasive in Hawaii, Florida

HABITAT
Forests, valleys, mountainous areas

DIET
Insects, plants

LIFE SPAN
5–8 years in captivity

The western diamondback rattlesnake lives across a wide swath of the American Southwest.

Spring has arrived in the New Mexican desert. Western diamondback rattlesnakes begin to stir from their months-long hibernations. They have spent the winter underground in natural holes or burrows made by animals such as prairie dogs. Now a male diamondback emerges from his lair, hoping to find a mate. In his search for a willing female, he comes across a rival male. They enter into a fight, but it does not involve bites or venom. Each snake stretches himself high above the ground, trying to prove to the other that he is the biggest and strongest. The challenger slinks away, allowing the victorious male to approach a basking female. He shows his interest by rubbing her head. She is receptive, and they mate for several hours. After 167 days of gestation, the female will give birth to anywhere from ten to 20 young. The babies hatch from their eggs inside their mother and are born live, a process that can take three to five hours. After staying with their mother until their first skin-shedding event, the young will depart in search of food.

RATTLES AND DIAMONDS

The western diamondback rattlesnake is one of dozens of rattlesnake species. It is found in the United States from central Texas to Southern California as well as through central Mexico. Its name comes from its range and the distinctive diamond-shaped pattern on its back. A typical western diamondback is tan or yellowish-gray with dark diamond shapes outlined in white. Eastern diamondbacks have a similar pattern but are found in the southeastern United States from Louisiana to North Carolina.

Western diamondbacks have a banded black-and-white tail that ends in the famous rattle. The rattle is made from previously molted skin. A newborn rattlesnake will have only a single button at the end of its tail. Once it has shed its skin, a piece will remain behind to form a second segment. Once it has three segments, the snake can rub the segments against one another rapidly to make the rattling noise. A western diamondback will add a new segment every time it sheds its skin. Because a snake may shed its skin multiple times during a year and frequently lose rattle segments as it ages, one cannot determine the exact age of a rattlesnake by counting the rattle segments.

DEADLY BITE

Western diamondback snakes are venomous, and they cause the most fatalities of any snake species in the United States. But they are not overly aggressive animals. Besides hunting, a western diamondback will strike only in defense. It will raise its body into an S shape, rattling in warning. This gives intruders the chance to move away. If the snake can escape, it will. Even if it does bite, some bites are dry, injecting no venom.

FUN FACT

A rattlesnake's fangs can get caught inside the prey. The snake can grow new fangs two to four times a year.[52]

The venom is useful for hunting prey. A rattlesnake has fangs that lie horizontally along the roof of the mouth when the mouth is closed. The fangs are covered in fleshy sheaths when they are not being used. When the mouth opens, the fangs swing forward and point out, allowing the rattlesnake to effectively stab its victim. Because the fangs fold backward, they can be longer than in snakes where the fangs are fixed and go deeper into the victim's skin. The snake's wide, triangular head holds venom glands, and the venom is injected into prey through the hollow fangs, which act like hypodermic needles. The venom kills the prey by causing loss of blood pressure and tissue destruction. Such tissue destruction actually represents the early steps in digestion, meaning the snake begins digestion of the prey item even before it is swallowed. Once prey has been subdued, the western diamondback will swallow it whole.

WESTERN DIAMONDBACK RATTLESNAKE
Crotalus atrox

SIZE
Up to 5 feet (1.5 m)

WEIGHT
Up to 14.8 pounds (6.7 kg)

RANGE
Central Texas through Southern California; into central Mexico

HABITAT
Deserts, rocky hillsides, scrublands

DIET
Small mammals, birds; sometimes other reptiles, amphibians, invertebrates

LIFE SPAN
More than 20 years in captivity

Greg Pauly, *right*, handles a dead yellow-bellied sea snake recovered in California in 2015.

Herpetologist Greg Pauly couldn't believe what he was seeing. The Pacific Marine Mammal Center had called him to collect a yellow-bellied sea snake that had washed up onto the shores of Newport Beach in Southern California. Yellow-bellied sea snakes live in tropical waters, and it was unusual to see them this far north. The northern end of their range in the Americas is typically Baja California, Mexico, more than 200 miles (322 km) to the south.

A person walking on the beach had nearly tripped on the snake before contacting the Pacific Marine Mammal Center. The center in turn called in Pauly, the associate curator of herpetology at the Natural History Museum of Los Angeles County. This was only the fifth yellow-bellied sea snake to wash up on California's shores since 1972. The others had all washed ashore during El Niño storm events. This one was different. Unlike most other sea snake

species, yellow-bellied sea snakes live out in the open ocean, carried along by currents. Scientists speculate that climate change is increasing the range of sea snakes by warming the ocean. Snakes can then get swept into currents that pull them out of their natural habitats into colder waters where they cannot survive. "On the one hand, I'm pretty excited that we've got yellow-bellied sea snakes showing up off the coast. As a herpetologist, that's kind of fun," Pauly said. "But the underlying cause is pretty terrifying."[53]

APPEARANCE AND BEHAVIOR

The yellow-bellied sea snake is one of dozens of sea snake species. It is found in the tropical and subtropical waters of the Indian and Pacific oceans, ranging from the eastern coast of Africa to the Americas from Ecuador to Baja California. It is the most widely distributed snake species on Earth. The yellow-bellied sea snake is completely aquatic. Its belly is V-shaped like the bottom of a boat, which helps it remain stable in water. This shape makes it unable to move on land. Its tail is flat, acting as an oar as it swims. Its dark back contrasts sharply with its bright-yellow belly, which warns potential predators of its toxic venom.

Yellow-bellied sea snakes spend much of their time at the surface of the water. Nostrils high on the snout allow the animal to breathe easily on the surface. These snakes can also absorb oxygen through the skin. They drink fresh water that accumulates briefly on the

A yellow-bellied sea snake eats a fish.

surface of the ocean during rainstorms before it fully mixes with seawater. Yellow-bellied sea snakes face little predation from other animals. Marine predators offered yellow-bellied sea snake meat in captivity often refuse the meat entirely or regurgitate it later, leading researchers to believe the meat itself could be toxic.

FEARSOME PREDATOR

Yellow-bellied sea snakes are ambush predators, lying in wait for fish before striking. They often suspend themselves among floating mats of seaweed or other objects on the surface. A small fish may approach a yellow-bellied sea snake, thinking the snake is debris. The snake might lunge sideways to catch the fish. If a fish is behind its head, the snake can even swim backward to get its mouth in range.

The sea snake's venom is vital for catching prey. A land snake can wound prey and stalk it while waiting for it to die. In the open ocean, sea snakes have no such luxury. They must kill prey quickly to keep it from getting away.

FUN FACT

Sea snakes have the most potent venom in the world, but due to their short fangs and small amounts of venom, human fatalities are rare.

YELLOW-BELLIED SEA SNAKE
Pelamis platura

SIZE
2–3.9 feet (0.6–1.2 m) long

WEIGHT
1.7–2.9 pounds (0.8–1.3 kg) for all sea snakes

RANGE
Indian Ocean, Pacific Ocean

HABITAT
Tropical and subtropical waters

DIET
Fish

LIFE SPAN
Approximately 2 years in captivity

REPTILE FEATURES

- All reptiles have scales, which are made up of keratin. This is the same protein found in human fingernails and bird feathers. Scales act as armor, protecting a reptile's skin and preventing water loss.

- Reptiles are ectothermic and cannot internally regulate their own body temperatures. They often bask in the sun to warm up and move into water or shade to cool down.

- Reptiles largely use lateral curvatures of the body to move. The exception is turtles, whose shells prevent lateral movement. They must use only their limbs to move.

NOTABLE SPECIES

- The saltwater crocodile (*Crocodylus porosus*) is the largest living reptile on Earth. It can live in both freshwater and saltwater habitats.

- The veiled chameleon (*Chamaeleo calyptratus*) can change the spacing of crystals beneath the skin to reflect different wavelengths of light. This allows it to change color to communicate with other chameleons.

- The green anaconda (*Eunectes murinus*) is the largest snake in the world, reaching up to 30 feet (9 m) long and weighing up to 550 pounds (250 kg). It kills its prey by constriction.

- Green sea turtles (*Chelonia mydas*) can go on journeys of thousands of miles when migrating from feeding to breeding grounds. A female green sea turtle will go back to the beach where she was born to lay her own eggs.

REPTILES' ROLES ON EARTH

Reptiles are found in temperate climates around the world, from arid deserts to tropical rain forests. They are not found at the poles. They play an important role in food chains around the world as both predators and prey. California kingsnakes (*Lampropeltis californiae*) keep populations of venomous snakes in check. Eastern long-necked turtles (*Chelodina longicollis*) are important seed dispersers, carrying seeds on their shells when they migrate.

REPTILES AND CONSERVATION

Reptiles are threatened by habitat loss, poaching, and introduced species. Tokay geckos (*Gekko gecko*) are poached for the pet trade or to be killed, dried, and used in traditional medicines. The Española giant tortoise (*Chelonoidis hoodensis*) was driven nearly to extinction by poaching and the introduction of new species to its Galápagos home. Captive breeding programs have helped restore its population. The tuatara (*Sphenodon punctatus*), similarly threatened by introduced species, has also been helped by breeding programs.

REPTILES AROUND THE WORLD

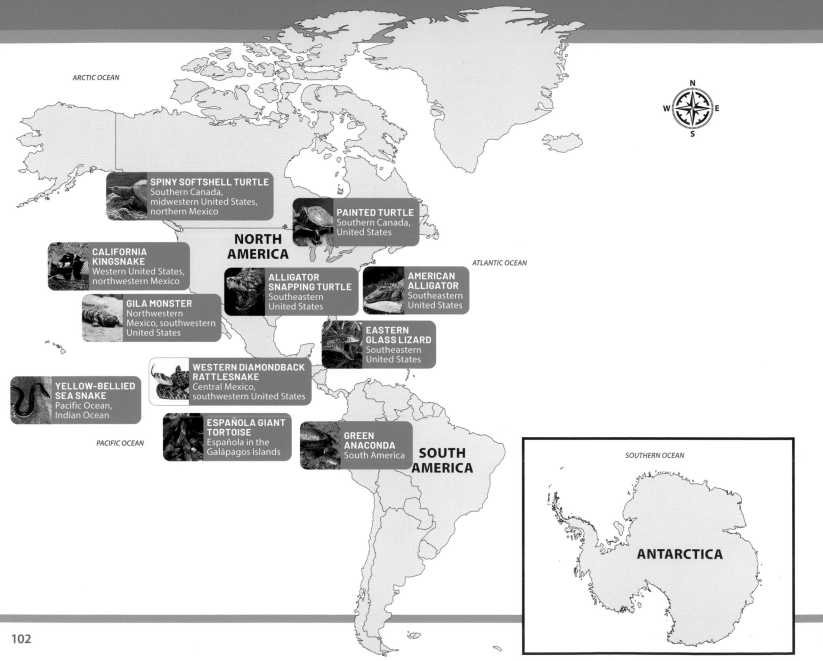

ARCTIC OCEAN

SPINY SOFTSHELL TURTLE
Southern Canada, midwestern United States, northern Mexico

PAINTED TURTLE
Southern Canada, United States

NORTH AMERICA

ATLANTIC OCEAN

CALIFORNIA KINGSNAKE
Western United States, northwestern Mexico

GILA MONSTER
Northwestern Mexico, southwestern United States

ALLIGATOR SNAPPING TURTLE
Southeastern United States

AMERICAN ALLIGATOR
Southeastern United States

EASTERN GLASS LIZARD
Southeastern United States

WESTERN DIAMONDBACK RATTLESNAKE
Central Mexico, southwestern United States

YELLOW-BELLIED SEA SNAKE
Pacific Ocean, Indian Ocean

ESPAÑOLA GIANT TORTOISE
Española in the Galápagos Islands

GREEN ANACONDA
South America

SOUTH AMERICA

PACIFIC OCEAN

SOUTHERN OCEAN

ANTARCTICA

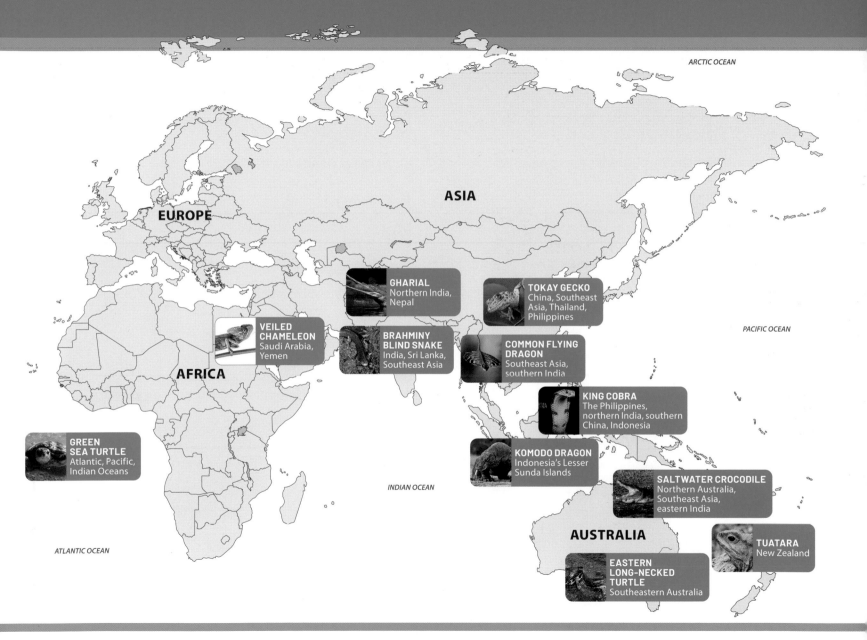

ARCTIC OCEAN

ASIA

EUROPE

GHARIAL
Northern India,
Nepal

TOKAY GECKO
China, Southeast
Asia, Thailand,
Philippines

PACIFIC OCEAN

**VEILED
CHAMELEON**
Saudi Arabia,
Yemen

**BRAHMINY
BLIND SNAKE**
India, Sri Lanka,
Southeast Asia

**COMMON FLYING
DRAGON**
Southeast Asia,
southern India

AFRICA

KING COBRA
The Philippines,
northern India, southern
China, Indonesia

**GREEN
SEA TURTLE**
Atlantic, Pacific,
Indian Oceans

KOMODO DRAGON
Indonesia's Lesser
Sunda Islands

SALTWATER CROCODILE
Northern Australia,
Southeast Asia,
eastern India

INDIAN OCEAN

AUSTRALIA

TUATARA
New Zealand

ATLANTIC OCEAN

**EASTERN
LONG-NECKED
TURTLE**
Southeastern Australia

GLOSSARY

biodiversity
The variety of species in a given area.

carapace
The hard upper shell of a turtle, tortoise, or terrapin.

carrion
The flesh of dead animals.

crustacean
A typically aquatic invertebrate with an exoskeleton and two pairs of antennae; includes crabs, barnacles, and shrimp.

El Niño
An irregularly occurring climate pattern in which warming waters in the eastern Pacific Ocean affect ocean currents, ocean temperatures, and local weather from Australia to South America and beyond.

endangered
At risk of becoming extinct.

flatwoods
Dry, low-lying areas with trees.

herpetology
The study of reptiles and amphibians.

HIV/AIDS
A virus and resulting disease that attacks the body's ability to fight infections; often spread by shared needles or unprotected sex.

incubate
To keep eggs warm until they are ready to hatch.

invasive

Describing an organism that arrives in a new ecosystem, takes over, and causes harm.

invertebrate

An animal without a spinal column.

mangrove

A shrub or tree with tangled roots that grows near the coast in tropical swamps that flood at high tide.

metabolism

The physical and chemical means by which an organism processes energy.

plastron

The part of a turtle or tortoise's shell beneath the body.

poach

To illegally hunt or capture an animal.

protein

An amino acid chain present in organic material, such as skin, hair, or blood.

scute

A large, bony plate; in turtles specifically, a piece that makes up the carapace.

subspecies

A group within a species that is able to breed with other members of that species but has genetic or other differences from those other members.

terrestrial

Of or relating to the land.

ADDITIONAL RESOURCES

SELECTED BIBLIOGRAPHY

"Animal Diversity Web." *University of Michigan Museum of Zoology*, 2020, animaldiversity.org. Accessed 15 Jan. 2021.

Kemp, T. S. *Reptiles: A Very Short Introduction*. Oxford UP, 2019.

Mattison, Chris. *Snake: The Essential Visual Guide*. DK, 2015.

FURTHER READINGS

Amstutz, Lisa J. *Bringing Back Our Freshwater Lakes*. Abdo, 2018.

Edwards, Sue Bradford. *The Evolution of Reptiles*. Abdo, 2019.

McCarthy, Colin. *Reptile*. DK, 2017.

ONLINE RESOURCES

To learn more about reptiles, please visit **abdobooklinks.com** or scan this QR code. These links are routinely monitored and updated to provide the most current information available.

MORE INFORMATION

For more information on this subject, contact or visit the following organizations:

The Field Museum

1400 S. Lake Shore Dr.
Chicago, IL 60605
312-922-9410

fieldmuseum.org/science/research/area/amphibians-reptiles

The Field Museum's Amphibian and Reptile Collection is one of the six largest herpetological collections in the United States.

Natural History Museum of Los Angeles County (NHMLAC)

900 Exposition Blvd.
Los Angeles, CA 90007
213-763-3466

nhm.org/research-collections/departments/herpetology

NHMLAC has a collection of approximately 190,000 amphibian and reptile specimens from around the world.

SOURCE NOTES

1. T. S. Kemp. *Reptiles: A Very Short Introduction*. Oxford UP, 2019. 4.

2. Kemp, *Reptiles*, 122–123.

3. "Lizard." *San Diego Zoo*, 2021, animals.sandiegozoo.org. Accessed 9 Mar. 2021.

4. "Galápagos Tortoise." *San Diego Zoo*, 2021, animals.sandiegozoo.org. Accessed 9 Mar. 2021.

5. Kemp, *Reptiles*, 4.

6. "Fishing with Alligator Snappers | Wild Mississippi." *YouTube*, uploaded by Nat Geo WILD, 30 Jan. 2012, youtube.com. Accessed 9 Mar. 2021.

7. "Alligator Snapping Turtle." *National Wildlife Federation*, n.d., nwf.org. Accessed 9 Mar. 2021.

8. Cindy Swirko. "If It's a Florida Body of Water, It Can Hold an Alligator." *Ocala.com*, 15 June 2016, ocala.com. Accessed 9 Mar. 2021.

9. Katharyn Seay. "Alligator Mississippiensis." *Animal Diversity Web*, 2019, animaldiversity.org. Accessed 9 Mar. 2021.

10. Seay, "Alligator Mississippiensis."

11. "Alligator Bites on People in Florida." *Florida Fish and Wildlife Conservation Commission*, Dec. 2020, myfwc.com. Accessed 9 Mar. 2021.

12. "Human-Alligator Incidents." *Florida Fish and Wildlife Conservation Commission*, Apr. 2019, myfwc.com. Accessed 9 Mar. 2021.

13. Van Wallach. "First Appearance of the Brahminy Blindsnake, *Virgotyphlops Braminus*, in North America." *IRCF Reptiles and Amphibians*, Aug. 2020, ircf.org. Accessed 9 Mar. 2021.

14. Masao Kamosawa and Hidetoshi Ota. "Reproductive Biology of the Brahminy Blind Snake from the Ryukyu Archipelago, Japan." *Journal of Herpetology*, 30(1), 1996. Accessed 9 Mar. 2021.

15. "Flying Dragons of the Jungle | Planet Earth II." *YouTube*, uploaded by BBC Earth, 16 Nov. 2016, youtube.com. Accessed 9 Mar. 2021.

16. "Draco." *Britannica*, n.d., britannica.com. Accessed 9 Mar. 2021.

17. Michael Van Arsdale. "Draco Volans." *Animal Diversity Web*, 1999, animaldiversity.org. Accessed 9 Mar. 2021.

18. David P. Badger. *Lizards*. Voyageur, 2002. 118.

19. Badger, *Lizards*, 118.

20. Ronald I. Orenstein. *Turtles, Tortoises, and Terrapins*. Firefly, 2001. 224.

21. Aimee Ortiz. "Diego, the Tortoise Whose High Sex Drive Helped Save His Species, Retires." *New York Times*, 12 Jan. 2020, nytimes.com. Accessed 9 Mar. 2021.

22. "Diego, the Galápagos Tortoise with a Species-Saving Sex Drive, Retires." *BBC News*, 16 June 2020, bbc.com. Accessed 9 Mar. 2021.

23. Orenstein, *Turtles, Tortoises, and Terrapins*, 175.

24. "The Biggest Tortoise in the World | Big Pacific." *YouTube*, uploaded by Discovery UK, 27 Oct. 2017, youtube.com. Accessed 9 Mar. 2021.

25. Ortiz, "Diego."

26. "Gharial." *National Geographic*, n.d., nationalgeographic.com. Accessed 9 Mar. 2021.

27. "Gharial." *IUCN*, 30 Dec. 2017, iucnredlist.org. Accessed 9 Mar. 2021.

28. "Monster Bites | Animal Armory." *YouTube*, uploaded by Nat Geo WILD, 16 Dec. 2016, youtube.com. Accessed 9 Mar. 2021.

29. Matthew D. Stewart. "Heloderma Suspectum." *Animal Diversity Web*, 2003, animaldiversity.org. Accessed 9 Mar. 2021.

30. "Gila Monster." *YouTube*, uploaded by USGS, 5 Aug. 2013, youtube.com. Accessed 9 Mar. 2021.

31. "Green Anaconda." *National Geographic*, n.d., nationalgeographic.com. Accessed 9 Mar. 2021.

32. Kendalyn Hersh. "Chelonia Mydas." *Animal Diversity Web*, 2016, animaldiversity.org. Accessed 9 Mar. 2021.

33. Hersh, "Chelonia Mydas."

34. "Brave Turtle – Australian Green Sea Turtle's Life Journey | Documentary." *YouTube*, uploaded by Docu Heart, 1 Mar. 2020, youtube.com. Accessed 9 Mar. 2021.

35. Chris Mattison. *Snake*. DK, 2015. 28.

36. "King Cobra." *National Geographic*, n.d., nationalgeographic.com. Accessed 9 Mar. 2021.

37. "King Cobra."

38. "King Cobra." *Fresno Chaffee Zoo*, n.d., fresnochaffeezoo.org. Accessed 9 Mar. 2021.

39. "King Cobra." *Smithsonian's National Zoo*, n.d., nationalzoo.si.edu. Accessed 9 Mar. 2021.

40. "Komodo Dragon Hunt Buffalo." *YouTube*, uploaded by Animal Wild, 2 Apr. 2020, youtube.com. Accessed 9 Mar. 2021.

41. "Komodo Dragon Hunt Buffalo."

42. Orenstein, *Turtles, Tortoises, and Terrapins*, 192.

43. Katie Knipper. "Chrysemys Picta." *Animal Diversity Web*, 2002, animaldiversity.org. Accessed 9 Mar. 2021.

44. "The Spiny Softshell Turtle: Ontario Wildlife Video Series." *YouTube*, uploaded by Ryan M. Bolton, 30 Sept. 2013, youtube.com. Accessed 9 Mar. 2021.

45. "The Spiny Softshell Turtle."

46. "Tokay Geckos in the Wild." *YouTube*, uploaded by Dav Kaufman's Reptile Adventures, 15 Feb. 2020, youtube.com. Accessed 9 Mar. 2021.

47. "What on Earth Is a Tuatara? | Modern Dinosaurs." *YouTube*, uploaded by Discovery UK, 9 Jan. 2019, youtube.com. Accessed 9 Mar. 2021.

48. Bruce Musico. "Sphenodon Punctatus." *Animal Diversity Web*, 1999, animaldiversity.org. Accessed 9 Mar. 2021.

49. Musico, "Sphenodon Punctatus."

50. "What on Earth Is a Tuatara?"

51. Alina Bradford. "Chameleon Facts." *Live Science*, 3 June 2016, livescience.com. Accessed 9 Mar. 2021.

52. Lisa Ingmarsson. "Crotalus Atrox." *Animal Diversity Web*, 2002, animaldiversity.org. Accessed 9 Mar. 2021.

53. Jason G. Goldman. "Venomous Sea Snake Found Off California—How'd It Get There?" *National Geographic*, 17 Jan. 2018, nationalgeographic.com. Accessed 9 Mar. 2021.

INDEX

Africa, 21, 37, 98
alligators, 5, 9, 16–19, 45
ambush predators, 12, 36, 74, 79, 99
Asia, 21, 60, 73
Australia, 21, 36–38, 73, 74

basking, 6, 48, 70–71, 78, 92
beaded lizards, 49
birds, 4, 5, 6, 9, 15, 35, 48, 56, 76
breeding programs, 40–41, 43, 46, 87
burrows, 48, 92

California, 26, 40, 93, 96–98
Canada, 69
cannibalism, 55, 85
capybaras, 52–53
carapaces, 13, 37, 41–42, 57, 70, 77
carrion, 36
chameleons, 88–91

classification of reptiles, 9
climate change, 5, 97
color changes, 7, 57, 82, 86, 88–90
constrictors, 24, 53
cranial kinesis, 26–27, 53
crocodiles, 6, 8, 9, 11, 18, 45, 72–75
crustaceans, 36, 74, 79

Darwin, Charles, 41
dewlaps, 28–30
Diego the giant tortoise, 40–41
dinosaurs, 5

earthworms, 20–21
eggs
   eaten by reptiles, 35, 48, 63, 67
   of reptiles, 14–15, 23, 30, 36, 43, 44–45, 46, 55, 56–57, 59, 62, 66, 68, 72–73, 76–77, 80, 84, 86, 93

endangered species, 43, 46, 57
Europe, 21, 86
eyelids, 33
eyes, 52, 74, 82, 91

fangs, 50, 61, 62, 94–95, 99
fish, 6, 13, 15, 36, 45, 74, 76, 79, 99
Florida, 17, 19

Galápagos Islands, 40–43
geckos, 6, 80–83
gharials, 9, 44–47
Graham, Terry, 38

hibernation, 39, 68, 71, 92

India, 21, 44, 46, 74
Indonesia, 28, 64
invasive species, 43, 89
invertebrates, 35, 37, 67

Japan, 23
jaws, 13–14, 16, 18, 25, 26–27, 35, 36–37, 45, 48, 52–53, 61–62, 64, 72, 74, 82, 86

Kemp, Tom, 5
keratin, 6, 14

legal protection, 5, 15, 46, 86
legless lizards, 33–34
lizards, 5, 6, 8, 9, 28–30, 32–35, 45, 48–51, 63, 64–67, 73, 80–83, 85, 88–91

medicine, 50, 81
Mexico, 26, 49, 93, 96
movement, 8–9

nests, 14, 19, 30, 44, 56, 62, 68–69, 71, 73, 74, 84
New Zealand, 9, 84–86
North America, 13, 17, 21, 68–69

parthenogenesis, 22, 66
Pauly, Greg, 96–97
pets, 5, 11, 15, 25, 80, 89
poaching, 46, 57, 77, 80–81
polymorphism, 25

relationship with humans, 4–5, 15, 19, 26, 40–43, 46, 50, 57, 80–81, 86–87, 94

San Diego Zoo, 40–41
scales, 6, 8, 20, 49
Schwalbe, Cecil, 51
scutes, 6, 37, 70, 77
sea snakes, 96–99
sea turtles, 56–59
seed disperser, 37
shedding skin, 21, 93, 94
snakes, 4–6, 8–9, 13, 20–23, 24–27, 32–35, 50, 52–55, 60–63, 74, 92–95, 96–99
Southeast Asia, 21, 73
subspecies, 41, 69–70, 78

temperature regulation, 6–7
third eye, 82
tongues, 12, 21, 25, 35, 48, 65, 91
tortoises, 6, 9, 40–43, 48
trees, 28–30, 48, 60, 66–67, 88, 90
Triassic Period, 85
tuataras, 9, 84–87
turtle necks, 36–39, 42, 78
turtles, 5–6, 9, 11, 12–15, 18, 36–39, 56–59, 68–71, 73, 74, 76–79

United States, 17, 35, 49, 69, 76, 93–94

venom, 24–25, 27, 50, 61–62, 65–66, 94–95, 98–99

Yemen, 88–89

ABOUT THE AUTHOR
K. A. Hale

K. A. Hale writes, edits, and designs nonfiction books for students of all ages. As a child she would spend hours in the pet store looking at snakes, disappointed that her mom would not let her take one home. She still thinks reptiles are fascinating and sometimes even cute. She lives in Minnesota and enjoys drinking tea, singing, and playing board games.

ABOUT THE CONSULTANT
Joseph R. Mendelson III, PhD

Joseph R. Mendelson III, PhD, is a professional herpetologist, specializing in frogs and snakes. His research in Central and South America has discovered dozens of species that are new to science. Reptiles and amphibians have been his passion since childhood. He lives in Atlanta, Georgia, and enjoys cooking, music, and traveling.